Six Contemporary French Women Poets

Leslie Kaplan

Michelle Grangaud

Anne Portugal

Josée Lapeyrère

Liliane Giraudon

Jacqueline Risset

SIX

Selection, Introduction, and
Translations by Serge Gavronsky

CONTEMPORARY

FRENCH

WOMEN

POETS

Theory,
Practice,
and
Pleasures

Southern Illinois
University Press
Carbondale
and Edwardsville

Library of Congress Cataloging-in-Publication Data

Six contemporary French women poets : theory, practice, and pleasures /
selection, introduction, and translations by Serge Gavronsky.

     p.   cm.

    Includes bibliographical references.

    Contents: Leslie Kaplan—Michelle Grangaud—Anne Portugal—
Josée Lapeyrère—Liliane Giraudon—Jacqueline Risset.

    1. French poetry—Women authors—Translations into English.

2. French poetry—20th century—Translations into English.

I. Gavronsky, Serge. II. Kaplan, Leslie.

PQ1170.E6S53   1997

841'.9140809287—dc20   96-41759

ISBN 0-8093-2115-7 (paper : alk. paper)   CIP

To Olivia,
a wonderful granddaughter

Contents

Preface

Novalis once said that it was nearly impossible to speak about poetry, and so, in defining this project, I decided to provide a set of questions to the six poets giving them total liberty to answer all of them, some of them, or none at all and substitute for the questions their own statements. In conjunction with the poets themselves, I decided that each poet and her poetry would be introduced with a very brief biography and a rather extended bibliography, listing her works in English where possible. In lieu of a bilingual edition, I opted for a larger selection in English.

My questionnaire included the following open-ended options:

1. What are the major French or foreign influences that have marked your work, including philosophic, literary, psychoanalytical, and filmic?

2. What do you consider to be the characteristic traits of your poetic writing?

3. What are some of the recurring themes in your poetry?

4. Does being a woman enter into consideration when you write?

5. Can you suggest any reason for the relatively poor showing of women in poetry anthologies in France?

6. What is the destiny of poetry as we near the end of the century?

Acknowledgments

I wish to thank the publishers Editions Gallimard, Flammarion, and P.O.L. for their permission to translate the following: Josée Lapeyrère, La Quinze chevaux (Paris: coll. "Poésie," Flammarion, 1987), 87–101, © Flammarion 1987; Leslie Kaplan, L'Excès-L'usine (Paris: P.O.L., 1983), 11–14, 70, 83–84, and Le Livre des ciels (Paris: P.O.L., 1983), 64–65, 72; Michelle Grangaud, Geste, Narrations (Paris: P.O.L., 1991), 7–20; Anne Portugal, Le plus simple appareil (Paris: P.O.L., 1992), 9, 13–26; and Jacqueline Risset, Petits éléments de physique amoureuse (Paris: coll. "L'infini," Gallimard, 1991), 9, © Editions Gallimard 1991. All other poems are translated by permission of the poets.

Introduction

Let me begin with what I believe is perfectly apparent to any reader interested in contemporary French poetry: women have never been as well represented in this literary genre as they have been in the world of fiction. In fact, to say they have been upstaged by male poets is an understatement. As of Plato and then throughout our Western tradition, men have always held a privileged position between the gods and humanity. They are the intercessors, the ones who are "inspired" from above. This quasi-sacred relation and ensuing responsibility—see Homer's first line in Robert Fitzgerald's translation of the *Odyssey*, "Sing in me, o Muse and through me tell the story"—has sidelined women poets.

And yet, from the Middle Ages to the present, women in France have never stopped writing poetry, though in our own century, to keep as close to the present as possible—women have still to occupy their rightful place in histories of French literature or, even more telling, in anthologies of poetry. It is precisely in such a gathering of poets that anthologists identify those who exist and those who do not. As far as the general public is concerned, and thereafter in selected translations of these same anthologies, the fact that so few women poets figure in these works may appear subjectively troubling, but the seal of authority of an anthology assures that such questions are usually ignored. Let me illustrate with two recent publications. The first is Robert Sabatier's massive three-volume *Histoire de la Poésie Française*,[1] where if ever a poet could be inscribed in this century, he or she would have won a place, and yet, the index reveals a remarkable paucity of women poets. When they are present, they never figure by themselves, defining a poetics or a particular mode of understanding poetry; rather, they are appendages, inscribed along the way with others in order to acknowledge their works without going into greater detail concerning their poetic production. A case in point is the space reserved for Jacqueline Risset, one of the six women poets included in this present work.[2] She is initially identified as the biographer of the French poet Marcelin Pleynet (665) and then, later on, as a remarkable translator from Italian into French, and vice versa, as well as a poet whose work is characterized by its "extreme condensation" (685). A quick glance into that table of contents reveals the preponderant place occupied by even such minor twentieth-century poets as Luc Estang or Pierre Oster Soussouiev. The list of male names could be vastly extended, but the facts are uncontrovertible: women have obviously not been acknowledged in this scholarly presentation.

My second and more recent publication is the *120 poètes français d'aujourd'hui* in which there are only eight women poets (Anne-Marie Albiach, Marie-Claire Bancquart, Andrée Chedid, Marie Etienne, Liliane Giraudon, Michelle Grangaud, Geneviève Hutin, and Anne Portugal). Three of these women poets are found in the present study. Thus, the first justification for my work would be to rectify a clear underrepresentation of significant contemporary French women poets. This task has been rendered easier by a most recent anthology *Poésies en France depuis 1960*.[3]

More specifically, the six women poets I have selected are not only significant as poets in their own right but representative of diverse interests characterizing French avant-garde poetry as a whole. By avant-garde, I mean to suggest the poet's commitment both to his or her own work as well as to an explicit desire to situate that work within a contemporary critical poetics, thereby providing readers with both text and context.

It should immediately be noted that in France, as of the beginning of this century, the avant-garde has been prominent in reassessing the relation between aesthetics and ideological positions (I am thinking here of dada and surrealism), in formulating radical political positions within a tradition-bound society (as did

Jean-Paul Sartre's existentialism), and in breaking with subjectivity and thematics (as did structuralism) in order to pay attention to the significance of form, language, and text as an autoreferential system. In each of the three examples above, one of the primary victims within the world of poetry has been the vestiges of romantic lyricism, fallen into disrepute, characterized by a lachrymose flooding and a solipsistic penchant. Each avant-garde movement has tried to recenter, in its own fashion, the place and significance of poetry, freeing it from the confessional abuses of a romanticism à la Alfred de Musset, for example.

If the six women poets hold their intellectual weight in the world of the avant-garde, or if one prefers, in the field of experimental work, it may also be attributed to the impact of the Tel Quel movement in the 1960s and 1970s, an impact of such persuasiveness that, clearly, not a single experimental poet escaped its lessons, however much these lessons have been in more recent years assimilated and even neutralized by a poet's own coming to terms with his or her needs as a poet and critic.

What then can be said of this central event in recent times? In the first place, one should acknowledge its double presence, as a magazine (with a provocative subtitle: Littérature/Philosophie/Science/Politique) as well as a collection published by Seuil. Were I to typify this group's contribution (a sort of latter-day Brigade or Pléiade) as succinctly as possible, I would insist on the framing of poetics within a philosophical, ideological, and linguistic order. By that I mean that poets and critics such as Jacqueline Risset (who was a member of the Tel Quel editorial board in the early days), Marcelin Pleynet, and Denis Roche, or prose writers and critics such as Jean Thibaudeau, Jean-Pierre Faye (who left the magazine to found Change), or Philippe Sollers, one of the principal voices in this revisionist enterprise, were all polemically intent on providing readers with a comprehensive analysis of the intellectual and artistic production founded on theories of classical thinkers such as Marx, Nietzsche, and Freud, and contemporary figures such as Claude Lévi-Strauss, Jacques Lacan, Michel Foucault, and Roland Barthes.[4] If this list of names is not quite sufficient to identify each of their contributions made over a period of time, the names themselves do indicate their primacy over the French intellectual horizon.

Tel Quel's insistence on rethinking past and present links between aesthetics, ideology, science, and politics was in line with André Breton's *Manifestoes of Surrealism* (1924 and 1930). It was also in accord with Sartre's systematic critique of bourgeois ethical and aesthetic values in his articles, in his magazine *Les Temps modernes*, as well as in his plays and philosophical works on Husserl, the imagination, Communists, Jews, and Arabs.

But added on to these nineteenth-century founding thinkers, Philippe Sollers and his friends proposed new interpretations of the grounding assumptions of French society. One can situate in this light the work of Louis Althusser who succeeded in separating the pre-1846 humanist Marx from his later structural analysis of capitalism; Jacques Lacan's use of Saussurian diachronic linguistics to bolster his contention that the unconscious was ordered like language, thus providing the analyst with rhetorical tropes as symbolic decoders of psychoanalytical symptoms; or the ethnographic work of Claude Lévi-Strauss and Roland Barthes's suggestive investigations into contemporary mythologies, both indebted to the pioneering work of the Russian linguist Roman Jakobson. Whatever was the particular point of departure, their efforts came to define patterns of underlying cultural significance no longer primarily dependent on a canonic insistence on meaning but on a semiotic reading of the ideological signs that constitute literary texts as well as "innocent" cultural artifacts. Without such support, the poet Josée Lapeyrère would not have been able to formulate the answers she provided me. Quite clearly, for her, the use of language, whether by a poet or an analyst, is not different: both must recognize the imperatives of the unconscious and the automatisms that bring them to light.

Had it not been for *Tel Quel* and that fermenting of intellectual activity, contemporary poetry would not have been the same. All experimental efforts passed through the trials by the language experience of the 1960s and 1970s, and thus, beyond their individual talents and their ways of seeing the world of the text as well as their own viewing of the world, one can conclude that the six poets here do, indeed, form a community of interest, sharing views in matters of poetics as well as in ideological and political ones. Furthermore, these six women poets are often found in the same magazines—*Action poétique, Banana Split, If,* and *Po&Sie*—as well as being published by P.O.L. and Flammarion.

How do these six poets resemble or, on the contrary, differ from their American counterparts? Let me illustrate what I have been noting above as a characteristic and ruthless critique of lyricism by quoting Maxine Kumin's introduction to *Anne Sexton: The Complete Poems* (Boston: Houghton Mifflin, 1982). In her preface, Kumin writes: "The stuff of Anne's life, mercilessly dissected, is here in the poems. Of all the confessional poets, none has had quite Sexton's 'courage to make a clean breast of it.'" And Kumin then goes on to affirm that "women poets in particular owe a debt to Anne Sexton, who broke new ground, shattered taboos, and endured a barrage of attacks" (xxxiv).

The difference between the French avant-garde and a lyrical American poetics could not be clearer: confessional poetry has been systematically associated with bourgeois tastes. With the possible exception of the surrealist poet Joyce Mansour,[5] the predominant rule for the six poets here included is one of restraint, of a measure of discretion, a rejection of the personal in too clear a poetic form.

I would add to this uneasiness with the confessional yet another strain marking aspects of mainstream American poetry, and that is an insistence on race and gender as definitions of one's identity. I am thinking of well-known poets such as Jane Barnes, June Jordan, or Audre Lorde. For the six French poets, one's sexuality per se is nobody's business, even though it may be profoundly present in the matter of the poem, as it is, indeed, in the works of Michelle Grangaud, Josée Lapeyrère, Anne Portugal, and Jacqueline Risset. The question, then, is not to conceal sexuality or gender altogether but to "play" with it as one would with a change of clothing taken from one's wardrobe. For the American poets listed above, life is the very heart and soul of poetry; poetry is a manner of confronting personal experiences and exposing one's wounds in that struggle. For the French, however, it is more a question of "life," that is, a distance taken from reality that allows for a more posed and at times ironic stance, even a humorous one. Everyone seems to agree with Wordsworth's formula that poetry is "emotion recollected in tranquility." The question, I suppose, is then the duration of that retreat from the world and the poetic line best suited to translate those emotions.

Do these six French poets have a corresponding presence in the United States, or must they somehow remain outside the pale of "reading"? Even a slight acquaintance with the poetry of Susan Howe, Diane Ward, Norma Cole, and Mei-Mei Berssenbrugge indicates a parallel commitment to form, sense, and language dictating the transmutation of "reality" into its other habitat called poetry. Perhaps the fact that many of these American poets have also translated contemporary French poetry is indicative of yet another line of communication between both sides of the Atlantic. I'm thinking of such well-known and up-and-coming poets as Rosmarie Waldrop, Cydney Chadwick, Cole Swensen, and Stacy Doris.[6] I do not suggest that there is a mimetic effect in play here but rather an affinity with the others' experimentation and a willingness to establish correspondences through translation: Tel Quel on one side of the Atlantic and L=A=N=G=U=A=G=E poetry on the other. If both influences have diminished, avant-garde poets who are anywhere from their late twenties to their late forties have most assuredly found inspiration in those two critical perspectives.

I would go so far as to say that given the national traditions of the avant-garde, transcultural resemblances have come to dominate to such an extent that, as the French poet Emmanuel Hocquard once told me, the distance is shorter between Paris and New York and San Francisco than it is between Paris and London. There is thus a true sharing of aesthetic ideological values that assure the six French women poets with an identifiable audience in the United States. This reception is all the more assured in what I recently referred to as a (re)turn to lyricism.[7] If young German poets like Sascha Anderson, Stefan Döring, and Bert Papenfuss-Gorek are once more attracted to word games, reminiscent of the dada period, the French, on the contrary, have stopped all such lighthearted endeavors; they have also forsaken an Oulipian mathematical formula dictating the choice of words and the ordering of the text in line with arbitrary rules that writers and poets such as Georges Perec, Harry Matthews, and Jacques Roubaud had so successfully applied to their writing.[8] If discretion, measure, and textual exigencies determine the writing of poetry, nevertheless, I find that the works I have selected are far removed from any formalist strategy, from any "objectivist" program as Louis Zukofsky's proponents in France had once practiced, and I am especially thinking of Anne-Marie Albiach and Claude Royet-Journoud.[9]

What does this (re)turn to lyricism signify? How is it rendered textually? In the first instance, it has always been there even when, as Roland Barthes had stated, only the syntactical "I" seemed interesting to him![10] Marcelin Pleynet's increasingly confident voice, stripped of its surrealist metaphors, is indicative of this, as are Jacqueline Risset's poems, perhaps the most "intellectual" of the six poets in this selection given her academic career and her critical writings on Bataille, Proust, and other major thinker/writers of our century. And yet in her poetry, the reader does not need much prodding to feel the emotions of love, of childhood, of loss. In the United States, this tendency has never flagged. One must only read the poets of the New York school to make sure of its continued existence—James Schuyler, Barbara Guest, Frank O'Hara, and, in particular, John Ashbery, whether in his 1975 Portrait in a Convex Mirror or in his recent Hotel Lautreamont (1992). The same is true for younger poets as well: Lyn Hejinian's 1987 My Life, Bernadette Mayer's 1985 Mutual Aid, or Abigail Child's A Motive for Mayhem (1989).

I now believe that even within the experimental mode there has been a remarkable reassumption of lyrical topics and, of primary significance, though certainly not the only topic to reemerge, love in all of its complexity. The body is no longer an abstract textualization but a presence, a wound, a joy. Reading Anne Portugal's representation of the biblical Susanna and the Elders is enough to convince us of that.

Before defining with greater precision the particularities of each of the six poets, it seems appropriate here to reaffirm certain aspects of a "community of interest," thereby further justifying the selection itself.

Not too long ago, a critic suggested that there are only two possible attitudes one can have when discussing language, either one of absolute confidence or one of deliberate suspicion.[11] That emphatic French position is both inappropriate here and highly debatable in its simplistic formulation. As a dialectical model, it may be a handsome way of proceeding in the abstract, but such a procedure does not conform to the specificity of the six poets in this presentation who, each in her own manner, propose a variation on a communal understanding of the place of language in avant-garde poetry. (Quotations from the poets are taken from the poets' answers to my list of questions to them, which may be found in the preface.)

Leslie Kaplan, referring to the importance of language in her work, calls attention to the "silence *within* words." This is indeed one of the key analytical traits not only of those six poets but of a general disposition in the avant-garde and its ongoing commitment to place language and problems raised by that field of inquiry at the heart of its preoccupations.

Malcolm Bowie, writing in the *Times Literary Supplement*, called our attention to the ever-widening gap between French and British poetry, using recent translations of the works of René Char, Yves Bonnefoy, Henri Michaux, and Philippe Jaccottet.[12] For the French poets, in one way or another, the ineffable lords it over the narrative, the descriptive, and the definitions of the relationship between the poet and everyday experiences, of that love and loss so perfectly incarnated in James Merrill's poetry or in England in Philip Larkin's or Christopher Logue's work.

If this metaphysical insertion into French poetry had once been symptomatic of avant-garde poetics,[13] under the influence of a poet like Hölderlin and a critic such as Martin Heidegger, I do not believe this is any longer the case. I would suggest that today times have changed, and though language remains a crucial issue in discussing one's poetics, the new element is one typified by a far more open consideration of everyday events that implies a (re)turn to a lyrical mode, to a subjective "I." Michelle Grangaud, describing her previous anagrammatic techniques, informs us that it meant a "transposition of the letters of a word or of a group of words in such a way as to form other words." If silence is no longer a basic motif, if, according to her own recent poetics, a play on words is still a dominant concern, she does add to that abstract technical operation the fact that the terms of the text thus constructed were neither erudite nor undecipherable: they were "working tools" that one could read without effort. It can easily be said that the elements raised in her anagrams touched upon the lives of human beings. Furthermore, as we near the end of the century, Grangaud believes that our poetry is in a "state of confusion" brought about by "historical and political questioning." I consider such a contextualization as indicative of the connection the poet draws between her own scrupulously defined lines of poetry and an overshadowing interaction with the world, a reality that is no longer contained in the text itself, in the anguish expressed by poets such as Paul Celan or in the writings of Edmond Jabès.

Anne Portugal expresses this connection in a metaphorical illustration when she asks "how to reduce—or restore—a savage luxuriance to the powerful geometry of a poetic space that is the urban site of our encounters." In her "public garden," there are people, leaves, fountains, and poems. Perhaps what holds all these disparate elements in place is "a question of rhythm, when we tighten it, where we let it go."

There is no denying it, words always hold center stage. One could argue that this has always been so, that poetry has always been a matter of words, made up of words, without which, there would be no poetry. That is assuredly a simplification of a highly complex understanding of the origin and function of words on the page, whether handwritten or printed.[14] Josée Lapeyrère agrees with Leslie Kaplan about the "silence," but in her formulation, poetry's task is to bring "to light a space . . . a language space, neither given nor guaranteed" but that the poet tries to reach "at all costs." Of all the six poets, she is certainly the one who has most thought about this space, which is shared by poetry and psychoanalysis in her case, since for her "both explicitly listen to sound and rhythm, linguistic equivocation, breaks in the line, cesuraes, scansions, that is to say, the effective dimension of time in language."

Where do these words come from? Liliane Giraudon's answers testify to their double origin—the literary one, ranging from Baudelaire through Emily Dickinson, as well as the closed universe of the poet. "One writes in order to be alone," declares Liliane Giraudon.

Jacqueline Risset's answer contains a sort of symbiotic proposal, incorporating the previous observations. She remembers Proust's 1908 Notebook that he wrote "in a state of urgency, condensed problems of experience, and the book to come." Or, as she recalls her own interests, she is definite about the site where they occurred: "I've always been particularly attentive to beginnings, to birth, to the initial instant when voice throws itself into the void." The incipit would then be similar to a jumping-off point, a privileged place from which all other things evolve. It is reminiscent of André Breton's assertion in the Surrealist Manifesto (1924) that the first word in an automatic writing exercise is always present and waiting to be called.

Clearly for the six poets, what is on the page is tantamount to tension, contradiction, and finally, in frequent instances, a resolution. Were poetry a question of transcribing one's personal experiences, a journal, a novel, or an autobiography might have done just as well. But poetry dictates its secretive orders to a closed/open universe, where words, as a consequence, have to be prudently selected, weighed, listened to, or again caught in the maelstrom of automatism.

For these reasons, all having to do with words, the six poets are perfect examples of a continuity with the great lyrical tradition of the past as well as with the schismatic experiences of the sixties and seventies.

If language represents the quintessential shared experience among the six poets, without a doubt, and indissolubly joined to the question of language, is the manner in which gender/identity is evoked through language. Once again, rather than uniformity, what exists is a panoply of interconnected responses to this very contemporary need to situate oneself not only within poetry but especially within the order of "outside-of-poetry" questions raised by feminists, literary critics, and readers, perhaps more responsive to ideology than to poetry itself.

"As far as women in poetry, I don't know," writes Leslie Kaplan. I interpret this apparently naive reflection as an unequivocal political statement, where decentering the sexual identity of the poet is a result of a literary/ideological focus on what truly matters, and that is as accurate a rendition of the "real" as possible. Let's not be naive ourselves! In L'Excès-L'usine, the women workers are of primary significance, especially in a world where traditionally the factory has been the fiercest representation of male capitalism. Thus for Leslie Kaplan her success is calibrated on the very absence of gender identity: a mode of "seeing" the others in their actuality rather than through one's all-too-clear insistence on self. I suspect that in the case of that collection of poems, if the poet muffles her gender, it is clearly meant to accentuate the gender issue linked to class concerns.

This is the strongest connection between the six poets. Grangaud turns it differently but in fact reaches the same conclusion when she wishes that she had never used her signature, wishing rather to have erased that gender sign. "How I regret not having thought of taking for a name my social security number." And she answers those who remain quizzical about her solution in the following way: "It seems to me that it is always the greatest absence of identity that produces the most powerful singularity in the case of a writer or a poet." The echo is clear: Mallarmé had stated the very same thing when he declared that the poet had to disappear in the poem. In fact, if there is a poem, it is because of the poem and not because of the signature; the form, contents, sounds, the rhythms, will or will not be convincing. Of all instances, in poetry the cult of the personality is ostracized. Is this a shying away from one's mirror image? Is Michelle Grangaud's poetics a form of self-effacement? Let each reader judge by the power of her lines where an ever-present sensitivity attests to a profound commitment to a reality indubitably shadowed by her presence as a woman. In the paradox of denial, presence is confirmed.

Anne Portugal echoes this situation when she claims that poetic space is a "space for vigilance against oneself, first of all, against the banalities of one's pitiful 'excellence.'" She then summarizes the question of identity: "Being a woman has nothing and everything to do with this." It is, in the first place, a poetic disposition: Portugal is not given to mimetic effusions of self-centered emotions, and equally significant, as she rejects what I can only refer to as the Sexton option, she recovers that particular ground by playing on a paradox that always sounds dadalike in its epistemologically disruptive refashioning of the "identity" question. Who am I? Portugal answers I am/am not a woman. As an "I" the signature must be valorized by what appears above it: there is nothing else to be concerned with. If a "woman" is immediately in play, then poetry itself is momentarily marginalized, and in its stead, "institutional concerns" take over, questions such as how many women figure in French anthologies of contemporary poetry? Or should women be better represented in this or that area of our society? Or closer to the act of writing itself, the matter of style that today, in a conservative French climate, seems to say: "Let's get back to good old-fashioned meaning, readability, religious aspirations, all of that in a bleached language, coded, in short, reappropriated."

Even as formalism diminishes, the language of poetry is again under attack by conservative advocates—by the very people who would wish poetry to repeat its nineteenth-century glories by accentuating the problems of the self in a language stripped of all pretension that is finding its way back to a clarity that prose exemplifies. To be lyrical would then be to fall prey to such ideological impositions; to insist on a "politically correct" staging of a poem in a woman's theater would be the equivalent, for an avant-gardist poet, of a form of betrayal. But as we shall see, the question is more delicate than that, and despite the facile association made between lyricism and conservatism, other strategies, borne of internal necessities within the theoretical confines of the avant-garde itself, have given rise to a (re)turn to that form of expression.

Josée Lapeyrère, in her own language, repeats this affirmation. For a poem to be faithful to itself, it owes it to itself to be clear and transparent, complex and paradoxical. "And for that, the poem owes it to itself to be 'cut up,' . . . according to what might be considered a torsion (as in a Möbius line)." This is an ars poetica, and it is inseparable from its author's claims that "at bottom, this means one would have to *change addresses* during the writing of a poem: letting go the old 'I,' the clichés, side glances, conventions." We recall Rimbaud's affirmation, "I is another," even if the woman surfaces at times: "Outside of love scenes of all kinds, as well as imaginary ones, i.e., directly linked to the presence or the evocation of a man, the feeling of being a woman plays a rather small part in my thinking, or so it seems to me."

How dull—that is, predictable—it would be if each poet, dwelling on the question of gender/identity, would duplicate an existing model! Liliane Giraudon provides us with a new twist when she declares: "I like the idea of being a woman *under the influence of*—traversed, shoved, cradled by diverse and multiple writings." And to the question concerning the place that being a woman plays in her writing, she responds with forthrightness: "As much, no doubt, as it plays within my body, but in ways that are much more complicated and multiple." And she goes on to state: "In any case, there's one thing I'm sure of: No writing is gender defined; there is no 'feminine writing.'" Would there be a more definitive formula? In her answer, I suspect Liliane Giraudon is also speaking for the other five poets who each on her own recognizes the obvious, that is, the gender issue, but considers as equally powerful the denigrating political reappropriation of their talents under the convenient label of a woman poet.

Jacqueline Risset comes to a similar conclusion by way of a distinctive preoccupation and particular textual allusions. Far from negating her "womanness," she considers it philosophically as a "supplementary game that defuses and impedes itself." For a critic who, early on in the company of Julia Kristeva and Jacques Derrida, reinterpreted the meaning of meaning in literary texts, it is not surprising to see her reach the following conclusion: "as of the feminine, the masculine is possible, but then so is the mineral.

Femininity considered not as continuity . . . but rather as a form of radical discontinuity, a new birth, absence of property, absence of law."

We are here far removed from a solipsistic insistence; the space of poetry is then one where gender vehiculates philosophical questions without turning them into autobiographies.

In evoking the six poets' definitions of self and gender, one cannot avoid appreciating a real "community of interests" evinced by these cumulative and reiterated principles upon which they all found their poetics: a sense of the autonomy of the text marked and unmarked by gender preoccupations, by a turn toward lyricism.

Lyricism was once coequivalent to poetry itself. It later became the object of radical criticism via automatic writing (a sliding from the "I" to the ego); in Sartrian theories of commitment, it was justified by leading poets writing patriotic sonnets during World War II; and most recently, in Tel Quel, it was rejected as a facile mode of writing, in fact, a way of writing that was exemplified by a kind of thoughtlessness that bolstered a prototypical association of the poet with the suffering romantic, an easily dismissible figure in the real world. Today that term has rid itself of both its conservative overtones (as a bourgeois fashion) and the unrestrained attacks on it led by such poets as Denis Roche who rather polemically declared that "poetry was inadmissible" (the title of his collected poetic works published by the Editions du Seuil in 1995).

If lyricism has made a comeback, that does not obviate the fact that in Leslie Kaplan's poetry there exists a rigorous demand on poetry imposed on it by a double theory of commitment—to politics as well as to poetics. She is thus a perfect representation of the persistent "intellectual" level found in French avant-garde poetry: both Maurice Blanchot and Marguerite Duras have admired her work. If gender, identity, and textuality find their place in her poetics, as they do in the poems of the other five poets, these themes do so with an extreme rigor that in Kaplan's instance bear on her ethical stance, her transgressive perspective on women workers in a factory, where they are not Chaplinesque figures but real human beings, exploited and suffering, with muted voices and bodies. If her poetry is all the more powerful, I would say it is due exactly to this artful combination of a vision of the world matched by her care for the text. To render perfect justice to the women in the factory, Leslie Kaplan has understood that an equally powerful, sustained, and measured voice was required.

This critical responsibility, a qualifying trait of the intellectual, combined with a deep concern for language, not as a tool for the transmission of "truths" but as part of the truth one wishes to convey, is fully observable in Leslie Kaplan's L'Excès-L'usine, poems written when, as a Maoist, she lived and worked with factory workers in January 1968.

Her experiences in 1968, as she describes them, are and are not within the scope of an anterior conceptualization of the role of the intellectual in French society. They clearly fall within a category of commitment, since Leslie Kaplan chose to live the life of a factory worker. The poems allow the reader to penetrate into the totalitarian system of the factory with its cruelties, its repetitions, and its boredom. The factory also serves as a metaphor for the life of women in a capitalist system. On the other hand, if one hopes to find Rosie the Riveter (a documentary made on U.S. women in World War II factories), one can only be disappointed, for the text is more in line with the sardonic criticisms of a Bertolt Brecht than with an outraged journalistic portrayal of reality.

As a result, even a first reading of L'Excès-L'usine complicates matters, since it leads one into a cinematic representation of daily routines and its antithesis, the stabilization of images, thereby countering Western philosophical understanding of representation, as well as a clear-cut Marxist interpretation. Transgression also makes its point poetically, since the factory and its excesses function as a symbol for the production of language and thus, besides the horrors of the place, the surface levels of the text— what I would consider as a form of communication in the first degree—Leslie Kaplan also provides a demonstration of a poetics at work.

In this manner, the poem reveals a double and interwoven message providing it with a weight that, I believe, characterizes all noteworthy avant-garde poetry. In reading her poems, the fundamental question is the *how* and its function; *how* the poem rarifies everyday language (a preoccupation among contemporary French poets), and *how* it strikes a balance between the obvious—the mirroring of reality—and its textualization, that is, the programming of a language adequate to the subject *and* to poetry itself. The incantatorial use of the impersonal "one" is an indicator of this reality/textuality choice that imposes a distance, a rigor, and a respect for those human beings transformed by an economy into factory objects of production.

Henceforth—and is not that one of the claims made by poetry itself?—it is impossible to avoid the presence of politics in both definitions: one playing on the traditional understanding of the term and the other, as it is applied to language itself, an expression of the political. The factory women become machines and inflect on Leslie Kaplan's language, as much as the women themselves carry such marks on their faces, their character, their sexuality. That is proof enough of the heightened effects on poetry that intellectual disciplines bring to the work itself.

Leslie Kaplan mentions the name of Serge Daney in her replies to my questions.[15] Founder of the cinema review *Trafic*, Daney (who died of AIDS in 1992) insisted that the primary function of the movie critic was to observe what was moving, a rather banal conclusion given the origins of that genre as motion pictures. And yet one might equally apply that concept to Leslie Kaplan as a poet and novelist. At every turn, and I mean to take that word also as a rhetorical sign as well,[16] one can see a poetics at work that, while according to the specificity of poetry its own rights, removes the barriers heretofore separating poetry from prose, aesthetics from politics. Her objective eye, her refusal to exploit subjectivity, her insistence on the polyvalent autonomy of the "seen," and, as a consequence, her desire not to exclude the aleatory explain the inclusion of flashes of the real (in all of her scenes) that help to construct a literary work as it screens the world, frees men, women, and children from an overly sentimental view.

The linkage of theory and practice is everywhere evident in Michelle Grangaud's textual universe. Here as I have mentioned, there is not the slightest outward sign of autobiography. On the contrary, one might even consider the use of anagrams, which she had so resolutely exploited in two previous collections of poetry, as her answer to a lyrical enterprise.[17] Much as the Swiss literary critic Jean Starobinski had analyzed the writing beneath the writing in Ferdinand de Saussure's texts,[18] subverting surface language in order to reach an underlying and more informative layer of meaning, so it might be said about Michelle Grangaud's early poetry that it successfully avoided the "obscenity" of a romantic posturing before an unknown public.

As a consequence of this intellectual manipulation of language, on the face of it, one could not find a more antithetical position to a feminist resolve than in Grangaud's work. Indicative of that is the reconstruction of anagrammatic meaning through a chance play of words constituting an apparent denial of the veracity of any initial demonstration. There is no doubt about this extreme form of restraint that her answers evoke with utter directness.

Again one might say that in her poems everything points to a concealed revelation, a mechanism that, with her aesthetics, confirms the impact of a *Tel Quel* influence in its insistence on a hermeneutical reading of existing texts such as the Marquis de Sade's or Lautréamont's. In her case, that influence can most readily be defined as a doubt cast on anything founded on the lyrical figuration of the "I." Such a distrust had been initially formulated by Nathalie Sarraute in her 1956 *Era of Suspicion*. This interpretation strips narrativity of a ready identification of author with narrator. Michelle Grangaud does indeed tell a story, but it is not specifically hers, and thereby she removes herself from the arena of anecdotal subjectivity. You will find in her anagrams no evidence of her daily life, her suffering, or those anxieties that have plagued her existence. And yet, in her long poem *Geste, Narrations*, as well as in her recently published poem "Rush,"[19] we are immediately confronted by the anguish that colors her intimate knowledge of a life composed of discreet units harshly defined, as if Michelle Grangaud had now managed to let us in on the secrets of a woman's life.

As much as the restrictive/liberating rules of the anagram,

perhaps here too it is the very presence of grids that permit such evidence to come to the fore and, in the first place, her choice of a light, pounding, reiterative structure. Throughout Geste, the poet maintains an even pace, as once distichs and monostichs had done. Here she opts for a triad, her own version of Dante's terza rima. This form gives her liberty of topic within a foreshortened syllabic count, reminiscent of the tanka. Exploiting this self-imposed logic, Michelle Grangaud describes giving birth, a highway accident, a lover's decision to leave, a woman applying her makeup. These Sappho-like fragments become all the more surprising when one realizes how they function within a system of alternation. Themes are blocked out, but they are not sequentially developed, so that they read as an unpredictable series of microchapters in a woman's life. One can also hear a musical scoring founded on slight shifts causing ripples, echoes at times (much as in twentieth-century experimental compositions), a degree of alienation, a cooling off due to her manipulation of rhythms. Structural breaks occur with irregularity—sometimes in the middle of a line, sometimes as an enjambment, sometimes scored by punctuation or the placing of a capital letter either at the beginning of a line or in the middle of it. To enter her poetry world is then to enter a space marked by consummate delicacy, power, and violence.

"I would like to be a stranger," writes the French poet Joseph Guglielmi.[20] As Michelle Grangaud refuses to claim her identity, that "I" that is not the poet's, she becomes Another, that is, woman/poet incarnate. Her repetitive, formal structure underlines a vision of movement, of the sweet terror of routine, of one's body and one's emotions. It might be said that a radical chaotic thematics emerges out of this scattering of triads, far truer to the essence of living than that compartmentalized order readers expect, especially when Aristotle's rules of logic are followed. In this rethinking of form and content, Michelle Grangaud reveals an absolute feminist-existentialist conscience, accentuated by her understanding of the role of the poet, and of a woman writing poetry in a world torn apart by wars and poverty.

To write in our time is audacious, perhaps impossible to think through, but it remains nevertheless the only act of courage left for anyone not able to plunge into the world's tragedies; or perhaps I should put it differently and state that the act of writing may be a more long-lasting commitment to the future of humanity than any single glorious or inglorious act.

Do we choose the life we lead? Can it be said that when we write about our lives that act not only corresponds to our truest selves, to the birth of words containing the totality of the abyss, of the disorder of the world, but also takes into account the impact of the world on ourselves? These doubts, reminiscent of a Sartrian postulate of the late 1940s and 1950s, may no longer be sufficient to calculate the passage from reality to the one drawn on paper; neither may these postulates be sufficient to explain the poet's exile, an exile at times glorified in Heideggerian terms where language—that opaque void, that frailty—struggles to reconstruct meaning out of an experience where a throw of the dice has little chance of ever abolishing chance.

In recalling the impact of theory, Anne Portugal makes a startling statement: Tel Quel experiences profoundly changed her character as a poet from a person with a baroque, even a kitschlike disposition, to one admitting to the disciplinary pleasures of those demands that theory considers a necessity when the act of writing begins. Theory is textuality's shadow.

The separation between oneself and one's poetic production is here joyfully acknowledged. In terms corresponding to her good humor, Anne Portugal explains how she delights in reading Jacques Derrida, even though she is not always sure about his meaning. This appreciation of the compressed duality in language—one given over to meaning and the other to music—is not as insouciant as it initially sounds. Derrida may be one of the finest poets writing in the French language today, since his écriture is the very proof of his theory of polyvalency, of a rejection of Eurocentric logic. There is a serious playfulness in Derrida's punning that explodes the myth of the singularity of meaning and that stipulates, as only the most effective poetry can do, the multiple resonances of meaning contained in a word, in a sentence. As an admirer of the French poet Francis Ponge, it is clear that for Derrida reason and resonance share the stage of écriture.

The ideological results of this devalorization of a single meaning (in line with Lacan's rejection of a unitary meaning contained in a subject's enunciation) is to throw conventional reasoning off balance, a balance that, philosophically speaking, implies the maintaining of a bourgeois order favorable to itself.

As far as poetry is concerned, this emphasis placed on writing formalizes the gap between what one may have perhaps too often called an American poetics founded on orality and a French one suspicious of the facility of the spoken register in written texts. In lieu of a poetic line shaped by a language that does not discriminate between the spoken and the written, in fact writes down the oral, as Allen Ginsberg does, the French avant-garde has insistently drawn a distinction between a spoken communication (and, let us say, the use of dialect) and the language of poetry that corresponds to another experience.

The clearest example of this difference in poetics, in gauging the importance of the spoken versus the scriptural, may be found in the opposition between a post-Whitmanesque Beat inspiration, with its incantatorial qualities, and, for example, Anne-Marie Albiach's verbal universe. There, and I am thinking of *Mezza Voce* (Paris: coll. "Textes," Flammarion, 1984), with a Mallarméan theatricalization (use of typography as figurations, spacing on the page as forms of choreography, repetition of lines as structured leitmotifs), *écriture* veils autobiography, though providing the text with a driving power all the more brutal because of its refusal to simplify the message therein. As the Beats perfected the art of public readings, and the concomitant emergence of a poetry designed for such performances, French poetics went into another direction exemplified by the poetry of Roger Giroux, Claude Royet-Journoud, and Jean Daive and by the prose works of writers like Roger Laporte, Louis-René des Forêts, and Edmond Jabès, for whom the spoken was translated into the aural. Clearly then, the French position, up through the 1980s, represented a critique of a nineteenth-century replay of the origins of poetry in the essential song, the epic poem, as well as in its soulful aftermath—an indiscriminate lyrical effusion.

Anne Portugal is perfectly conscious of this contending poetics, of this French stance in her own work, but, as always with the poets here represented, there is a subtle reorientation given to these theoretical formulations. One can see this in Portugal's poetry, in line with her contemporaries, where the blocking of the text on the page is already a statement in and of itself. In one of her recent books of poetry, *De quoi faire un mur* (Paris: P.O.L., 1987), the insubstantial quality of the italicized poem on the left page (but not all left pages are so identified) suggests a series of translations: from obscurity to light, from past to present, from memory to recollection, from sotto voce to plainsong.

Consequently, the poems are, and are not, easily accessible, much as medieval women poets (the "trobairitz"), could opt for *leu* or *clos*, an open or closed poetics. But then again, Anne Portugal might reply, why indeed write "easy" poems. If Derrida constitutes a propaedeutical approach so, in their own way—or is it simply the way of poetry?—do Portugal's poems. The reading of them, the mouthing of them, and, of course, the meanings in them make of them enticing rewards. It might then be said that experimental poetry in France exemplifies a union that enriches both poetry and the readers, making of sound an emblematic carrier of meaning and of meaning a support for sound.

Specifically, Anne Portugal, interested in theory, self-effacing on the surface, nevertheless, and with tongue in cheek, goes much further than male painters (Tintoretto, Veronese, Masson) have done when she recuperates the biblical figure of Susanna and finds analogies between her beauty, the two lecherous old men, and the expropriation through the male gaze of that woman, which has become, both in Christian iconography and in Western painting, one of the telltale signs of the objectivization of woman. Susanna is thus a figure in Anne Portugal's fascination with the Bible as she becomes a litmus test of beauty as well as an homage rendered to poetry itself. In this fashion, Portugal continues a tradition that can be traced all the way back to the trobairitz.[21] Woman as double subject: praised and honored in life as she also becomes the exemplum of poetry. In love poetry—but what else is going on in Anne Portugal's relation with poetry itself?—one is always aware of the artist's attention, through the figure of the woman, on the poem itself. All poetry, finally, is an homage rendered to language.

This recognition by poets of poetry and its antecedents goes further when one reads the answers given by the six poets. In many instances, Emily Dickinson and Gertrude Stein appear, and to this short list, one should add Anne Portugal's evocation of Sylvia Plath when she writes: "dans le plat/de Sylvia/déjà froid."[22]

What seems to me increasingly characteristic of poetry in French avant-garde circles is its internationalization through a reading of poetry in translation. More than ever, there exists a fascination with not only works by classic American poets, such as Pound and Zukofsky, but also recent poetry written by the American avant-garde.

Anne Portugal also mentions (as does Josée Lapeyrère and especially Liliane Giraudon) the Russian poet Marina Tsvetayeva (1892–1941). Therein lies an informative footnote to the discourse on contemporary avant-garde poetics. One of the major lyrical poets in the former Soviet Union, Marina Tsvetayeva, until quite recently would have been more abhorred than admired as a model for avant-garde poetry. Today the tables are turned, and she has become a weather vane of that (re)turn to lyricism in France.

The reasons for her posthumous acclaim are due to a complex set of facts, including her nationality, her poetics, the content of her poetry, and the play of gender. In the first place, her Russianness: her language, her traditions (including a touch of that illusive Russian "soul"), her friends and lovers (among whom numbered Ossip Mandelstam and Alexandr Blok as well as another poet, Sophia Parnok), and the horrific historic epoch through which she lived and died, committing suicide in 1941 when the Soviet Union was invaded.

Her success may also be attributed to a tinge of nostalgia for the former Soviet Union on the part of the French left and especially on the part of present members of the French Communist Party, among them Henri Deluy, a poet himself, who edited and translated the 1992 *Marina Tsvetaieva: L'offense lyrique*[23] and included in that work a prefatory essay on her life and work. Editor in chief since 1954 of the influential magazine *Action poétique*, Henri Deluy is now also, together with Jean-Jacques Viton and Liliane Giraudon, coeditor of the Marseilles-bound magazine *If*, whose first issue was devoted to Deluy's translations of the Russian poet.[24] But it is in his essay that Henri Deluy defines his own—and perhaps the group to which he belongs—ambivalent feelings when he first read Tsvetayeva's poetry, which she herself describes as her "intimate journal."[25] After all, was not her style and the origin of her inspiration the very incarnation of that perverse tendency his circle had fought against for so many years? And yet, almost begrudgingly, he admitted that her poetry was so powerful that it not only surmounted any possible theoretical hesitations but, as I see it, actually seemed to have liberated an equal charge of lyricism, prior to this moment sublimated for years in avant-garde circles. In her own homage to the poet, Liliane Giraudon declared that as we near the end of the century, Marina Tsvetayeva represents a mass of energy that acts as a precious source of nourishment.[26] That "nourishment" is composed of a lyrical excess, the measure of a clear autobiographical narrator, and the poetization of her love affairs together with her joys and numerous sorrows (in fact, much of that is to be found in American poetry). For a "dépassée" poet, Marina Tsvetayeva has marvelously succeeded in imposing herself, her style, and her themes.

If Anne Portugal and Liliane Giraudon express their admiration for that Russian poet and her life, the reasons may also be due to the waning of a militant direction in French feminism. After the activist period defined by Simone de Beauvoir through Simone Veil's abortion legislation in the 1970s, French feminism may be on the lookout for new models, and I would suspect that that too enters into the decision to include the Russian poet in a sisterly Pantheon. Lastly, but here I may be stepping out on a limb, I would think that Marina Tsvetayeva offsets a commanding lead that contemporary American women poets have, whose works are being translated into French.

If theory in poetics has played a defining role in the work of the three poets so far analyzed, this coupling is all the more suggestive in understanding Josée Lapeyrère's poetry. In her case, as a practicing psychoanalyst and poet, one can evoke a double-theo-retical program. In the first place, she adheres to a poetics that systematically excludes any sign of a traditional narrative process; she equally banishes versification from any of her concerns—con-cerns that in Paul Valéry's *Art poétique* were meant to facilitate the poet's task. These are discarded in the name of a modernity that adopts the strategies of the unconscious, the unpredictableness of verbal substitutions functioning according to a semantic slid-ing also justified by sonorities. Such surprises assure the forward propulsion of the poem.

In the absence of traditional preoccupations, time and again Lapeyrère insists on the importance of structure and, in particu-lar, on a theoretically weighed practice of line breaks and breaks within the lines of the poem itself. They are the true mechanizing principles of the text and not the themes that float above these structural constructs. Thus the poem, though rejecting preexist-ing conventions, contains, nevertheless, an aesthetic ideal founded on the haphazard doubling of meaning, as Freud had analyzed it in his *Jokes and Their Relation to the Unconscious.* Her practice as a poet also recalls André Breton's idea of a fortuitous encounter, of a jostling of word images that automatic writing transcribes as the "true functioning of thought." But here again, Breton stands corrected. The emergence of the word may be unsuspected, but its later trajectory is ordered by the poet; there is no doubt about this maneuver.

Thus one might conclude that Josée Lapeyrère sides with that antagonist defined in Boileau's seventeenth-century *Art poétique.* Not only does she dispel the myth of classical versification and the seduction of logic, rather central for most poetry, but in recogni-tion of the play of chance in the wording of the text, she happily falls into that folly Boileau had assigned to the Italians. As that classical poetician had restricted folly to those baroque trans-Al-pine poets, so he developed for his own countrymen a poetic justification founded on a rational chain of meaning. It is against this ingrained French tradition that Josée Lapeyrère reacts when she shifts away from a Cartesian meaning to a poetic line ready to welcome surprises of a sonorous and rhythmic nature. As Saint-

Pol-Roux expressed it, the poet is at his best when he is asleep in an active-passive condition that allows the poet, in a dreamlike trance, to harvest a season of images. These images reform meaning according to a nonlinear, non-Aristotelian mechanism.

One should note, however, a crucial ideological distance between Lapeyrère's work and surrealism's optimal utopic reconciliation of opposites, of considering itself as a para-Christian promise of an earthly paradise—a sort of absolute ecology where men, women, and sometimes children would once again find themselves in harmony with nature. I do not believe this surrealist optimism, in a fusion attained through love or language, is shared by Lapeyrère. Rather, she is indebted to a confrontational questioning of conventional concepts of meanings that, paradoxically, has made it quite clear that those who adhere to them support naturalism in the novel and legibility in poetry. In this context, there is nothing more consequential than Rimbaud's own observation in answering his mother's query about the meaning of the poems in *La Lettre du Voyant*: "It says what it says literally and in every which way."[27] Lapeyrère's poetry and her psychoanalytical training would find a justification in that comment.

If part of Lapeyrère's redefinition of classical poetics comes from surrealism, though downgrading its metaphysics, it also comes from one of surrealism's cherished objective correlatives: Freudian psychoanalysis. For Lapeyrère, there is one further step to take, and that is to ascribe to the unconscious appearance of words a telling significance.

Though I am making a division between two sets of assumptions, one founded on poetics and the other on psychoanalysis, in Lapeyrère's understanding of poetry, the two share a chiasmic relation, since both, though with different goals in mind, operate according to similar perspectives—both listen to the sound and the rhythms of language, to the equivocation of language and its indeterminacy, together with those pauses introduced in a spoken or scriptural landscape that allow the reader or listener to scan the lines for meaning. To these basic determinants, Lacan added the audition of rhetorical figures but especially—and here Lapeyrère is in concordance with Lacan—the extraordinary meaning of what initially appears to be nonmeaning. This level of language, unattainable through discursive means, invests the text, poetic or delivered by a patient, with unsuspected significance. After all, it is in language, through language, and about language that poetry makes itself known and not—as some would have it— as a transparent verbal copy of the world. It is also within language that the patient exists, that his or her patience is tried as an apparent "other" voices the verbal contents of the dream.

Josée Lapeyrère thus grounds her definition of poetics and of poetry on the principles of a thoroughly articulated theory of language as well as on the relation between language and meaning, a language chain momentarily broken off from the linear evolution of conventional practices, open for a time being to the inscription of new words, new meanings. By now, it must be clear that her poems exist on two levels: her discourse on poetics suggests an initial illegibility, while her texts appear perfectly clear to the first reader who comes upon the scene of her writing. However much the juxtapositioning of words may be disturbing, her poems also afford great satisfaction and pleasure of a "traditional" nature.

When the Egyptian-born French writer Edmond Jabès wrote about meaning in meaning and assumed that memory canceled itself, though remaining accessible in words, Lapeyrère goes one step further, since it is in the sounds and the rhythmic patterns that memory, without ever being named, exists. Language, as a signifying practice, whatever its surface meanings, evokes memory through the echo system of language.

Closer to Freud's theories on screen memory, Josée Lapeyrère understands that words harbor words, that puns expose unwanted meanings and perhaps truer than the ones we express. The poem would then be analogous to a patient's recitative in a psychoanalytical session or again equivalent to the Delphic oracle. Through the mouths of words emerge other words, and these have weight and bearing beyond our initial and censurial understanding of them. Josée Lapeyrère does not speak about the unconscious, nor does she value the translation of "pure thought" as Breton had once defined it in his *Surrealist Manifesto*; she is, however, most precise about the mystery of the unintended surging of meaning, of ascribing to pauses a kind of shamanistic importance. As one deciphers the partitions of the poem, as individual lines are broken up by variable pacings—two, three, or more spaces between words or two, three, or more double spaces between groups of lines—the poem slowly comes to form a totality.

As I reread the above, there is yet another level, one that any reader sees without any difficulty, and that is the ambivalent portrayal of the symbolic identities of a woman's life. Whether she describes sexuality in clothing, the erotic in everyday life, the act of washing dishes, or, by a mythic association, an evocation of apples, Lapeyrère's representations are always the recognizable indexes of a poetry written by a woman. Thus the openness of what Barthes called "the doxa" (public opinion),[28] and what Lapeyrère proposes as a para/doxa, or an alternative system of perception. She recuperates feminine stereotypes, explodes clichés, gives polyvalent amplitude to the text, and as a result, the reader is made aware of what women have borne, have assumed, and, ultimately, have discarded.

Liliane Giraudon is interested in yet another and—at least in France—little-tolerated topic, and that is writing on female sexuality. This is apparent in her prize-winning short stories *Pallaksch, Pallaksch* (1990) where, through shifting scenes, the object remains the same: the relation between women and men, between women and animals, between women and the space they occupy whether urban or agrarian, a reminder of Liliane Giraudon's early years in the country. But the disjunction between Liliane Giraudon's approach and, let us say, popular literature written by women is that *écriture* comes into play with a ferocious autonomy. Liliane Giraudon is as exact in the confrontation between thought and language, thought and syntax, thought and rhythms as any poet would be listening to lines of narration. Indeed, when writing prose, Liliane Giraudon remains primarily a poet, someone particularly attentive to spoken and written language.

In recent years, the canonicity of the separateness of literary genres has preoccupied Liliane Giraudon. For her, it is literally impossible to think about poetry or prose as noncommunicating vases. If her prose is founded on a poetic attention to language, poetry itself cannot exist as a privileged entity, an elitist one, hovering over reality, somehow outside a political/public discourse. Writing poetry today may be inadmissible, to quote Denis Roche, but if there is a way out of this impasse, it must be in the recasting of poetry's identity and, as does Liliane Giraudon, assume that poetry is only feasible when it incorporates fragments of letters, prose texts, interrupted narrations, that is, all the signs of modernity that one can find in Louis Zukofsky's poetry. This is evident in the tone and content of her long poem that I have translated and that doubles as a poetics wherein, coldly and passionately, she defines through the writing of the poem itself what a poem should be.

Saying that, one might suspect that meaning in its classical sense had been evinced from her writing, but that would be far from the truth. Indeed, meaning dominates Liliane Giraudon's work. The audition of layers of residual meanings or the grasping at unconscious messages in flight is not at stake in her poetry. Should one ascribe this positivist turn of mind to her early training with Catholic nuns? Should it be associated with a later politically committed view of the world? The fact is that in Liliane Giraudon's prose and poetry, a continuum is assured by a clarity of intention, by an exquisite working of language and syntax. The battle is joined; to oppose a contemporary move to the political right, and especially to an abject return to antifeminist positions in France, she has had to redouble her efforts in writing, as she has multiplied her meetings with women whether in Egypt, Russia, or France. If the impact of feminism has weakened in France, for Liliane Giraudon the fault is not so much in the enemy's offensive as it is in feminism's own decision not to go further, and that means confronting the very demons of bourgeois mentality: the possibility of literature turning itself into a cannibal, threatening the status quo.

Of all the women poet/writers I know in France, Liliane Giraudon is the one who most systematically accuses the reigning "virtues" of genre classification. This is done not in the name of a new aesthetics or counterpoetics but in the name of a new alignment of literary production with a political consciousness, where such a preoccupation has been, for the past thirty years, sidelined by structuralism, by theories emphasizing linguistics rather than Marxism, existentialism, and feminism. Is it because Liliane Giraudon, who taught school in one of the worst North African neighborhoods in Marseilles, had the opportunity of listening to her students as they told her horrendous stories of rejection, discrimination, and a life condemned to mediocrity? She prizes these stories but will not introduce them directly into her work, since she considers such information a privilege based on an ethical contract that forbids such experiences from being turned into literature.

Perhaps it is this questioning of literature that is yet another common ground on which the six poets establish their interconnection—a refusal to accept the rules of poetry, a refusal to accept a romanticized and edifying solitary confinement for women poets.

This questioning becomes the marker for avant-garde projects and especially in Jacqueline Risset's poetry. It may most accurately be said about her that a vibrant juncture exists between her critical discourse and her creative work. At no time has this juncture been frayed. It began in the period 1966–83 with *Tel Quel* to which she contributed texts on literary criticism and the theory of translation. After her departure from both *Tel Quel* and Paris, she established herself in Rome where she is now professor of French literature at the University of Rome and continues her work as a critic, poet, translator, and sometime journalist.

Jacqueline Risset's evolution from those early years during which she worked at *Tel Quel* to her recent collections of poems is indicative of that reorientation of poetics to a (rediscovered) lyrical voice. One might even consider this passage as a sign of the radical transformation in her aesthetics. She remembers that in the old days her poetry was "enigmatic, elliptical, anti-autobiographical"[29]—so much for the 1960s through the early 1980s. Something occurred to change that understanding of poetry, and for Risset, the turning point was a decade spent in translating Dante's *Divine Comedy*. The effect of that lengthy immersion into medieval poetics has been to change her language as well as the content of her work into a much more accessible form—simpler, more direct and autobiographical. In line with Proust and Freud, Risset has been propulsed by the authenticity of a return to childhood, of love, as she then felt it and later could reformulate it in adult terms.

Such a personal shift is emblematic of the new directions in contemporary French avant-garde poetry. In *La poésie n'est pas seule* (1988), Michel Deguy's thesis can be applied to Risset's work, since she is at once poet, translator, and critic, and nothing allows a hierarchical classification to stratify these three constituent elements. Such a conjoining of elements permits the reader to understand that writing a poem is not the result of chance, or worse, of an inspirational surge, as Plato would have it. Rather, poetry is the sum total of one's intelligence and sensitivity, of one's ability to listen and then to correct such thoughts or sounds that have come from an "elsewhere." There is no branch of knowledge Risset has touched that has not fed her poetic work, and I would say that that includes Roman Jakobson's views on linguistics as well as Dante's poetics and one of his primary concerns— love, which is so assiduously followed in the *Divine Comedy*.

To understand Risset's poetics is then to come to grips with *Tel Quel*'s enduring intellectual pronouncements: an updating of Freud's work in the light of Saussurian/Lacanian linguistics; a rereading of Bataille's works; a signal importance accorded to semiotics in its Barthesian application. Reading her poetry, her miraculous translations from the Italian, and her critical essays, one quickly sees both the continuity with the past as well as a highly personal rethinking of its basic premises.

Lastly, I would like to go back to that medieval poetics of the trobairitz and draw a line joining it to contemporary French poetry in order to suggest that Jacqueline Risset is the truest descendant of those first women poets who were at the inception of the writing of poetry in France.

In order to speak about Risset's indebtedness to that period, one must recall that anterior poetics, which was founded on self-referentiality, on a poetry mirroring itself, also found solutions that would have poetry reflect an individual's sensitivity to the world. Paul Zumthor showed that the accomplishment of language and form typified the work/pleasure of medieval poets.[30] If Risset now voices hitherto questionable lyrical themes, it is in line with Rimbaud's dictum in *La Lettre du Voyant*—that one has to find a new language to express such thoughts, such feelings.

The effects of these rich sources of inspiration are as apparent in her Dante translations as they are in her *L'amour de loin* (1988) that replays some of the lessons of medieval poetics, including the major thematics of courtly love, of the poet inscribing himself/herself in the ritual of the poem itself. But in that work, the connection is even more blatant, since hers is the very title of one of Jaufre Rudel's thirteen-century works: *La Chanson de l'amour de loin*. As if that were not enough, Jacques Roubaud, in his *La fleur inverse*, devoted a section to the analysis of that question and concluded: "Le spectre des troubadours hante la poésie."[31] One could then say that if Risset writes love poetry unlike that of her nineteenth-century precursors, she does, on the other hand, and quite faithfully so, follow in the wake of the trobairitz. We are obviously at a considerable distance from poems written by the Comtesse de Noailles who continued, in the most classical forms, to express her romantic aspirations. Risset's love poems are also as distant from the violence of Joyce Mansour's anatomically explicit texts as they are from the philosophical works of a Catherine Pozzi.

What then can be said about her love poetry? On the surface, it appears to parallel a recuperation of the affective in avant-garde poetics, no mean feat given the ejection of thematics in general and of love in particular. With the possible exception of Marcelin Pleynet's erotico-Oedipal reminiscences,[32] one must turn to her poetry to find a subject so infrequently pursued by her contemporaries. She has set before herself a venturesome task, and the fact that she finds it a necessity is proof enough of the authenticity of her commitments. How much more radical can her decision be, given the very low esteem contemporary critics and poets have had for "authenticity" in literature, a carry-over of a nineteenth-century vision according to which, and in line with Rousseau and Chateaubriand, poets and writers unloaded the "truth" about their lives in their fiction and poetry.

In *L'amour de loin* as well as in her *Petits éléments de physique amoureuse* (1991), Risset expresses the inexpressible. This can only be tolerated when filtered through a poetics recalling the trobairitz, for it is in that tradition that such poems can be written today, a tradition representing a dual insistence on emotions and textuality. If her versification does not rival with that archly demanding poetics developed in the Middle Ages—though her uses of typography, spacing, and punctuation are a reminder of a parallel enterprise—she does renegotiate that contract that, for lack of a better word, we call form and content. As of the title *L'amour de loin*, one is forewarned that the referents are literary, historical, and poetical. The title unambiguously stands for courtly love. But thereafter, each poem can be read as a sign of Risset's personal experience as well as a testimony to her culture—these are poems of love and death, of suffering and joy, that pay equal attention to poetic space. In this way, the texts settle within a tradition and its renovation.

The problematics of love are even more elaborately treated in *Petits éléments de physique amoureuse* where she provides an introductory essay, "L'amour de la poésie" (a reworking of Eluard's *L'amour la poésie?*), that sets the book in motion, guiding the reader through the labyrinths of her affections, as she evokes the instants seized in her poems, which, as of the first page, explicitly define a troubadour belief that to sing and to love are synonymous verbs. Yet Jacqueline Risset modifies the concept of distance by assuming that writing a poem, as it distances oneself from the object of the text, actually raises our expectations. All the pores of our body are thus brought into play in this physique of love or, as she phrases it in her poem "Perfect Love," that "Perfect love [that] opens life/back to childhood." Though the trobairitz would most likely have avoided such a Proustianization of the text, they certainly would have agreed with Risset in her English-titled poem "Spring Flower" that begins: "Four and a half years of pure love." Distance, textuality, and the courtly tradition of love—these are the elements of that medieval trinity

found in Provençal poetics that, unexpectedly, have been success-
fully resurrected in her poems.

In writing about the avant-garde, the temptation has frequently
been to find a prose as obfuscating as some of the texts them-
selves. In reading the six French women poets, I hope I have
avoided such a stylistic pitfall. Their poetry revels in light and
challenges the reader with a need to rethink clichéd definitions of
the avant-garde. There are new themes abroad, as I have pointed
out throughout this introduction; there is an exemplary pleasure
expressed in these texts in opposition to a much somberer, terror-
istic-theoretical penchant in the sixties and seventies; these po-
ems chide past assumptions as they too manage in often unexpected
ways to combine once again the poem with its accompanying
theoretical formulation. In reaffirming the participation of women
as poets, I believe I have reconnected today's work with an im-
memorial tradition that in France clearly goes back to a Middle
Ages rediscovered by the surrealists and, filtered through the *Tel
Quel* experience, emerges today as one of the strongest and most
enjoyable textual experiences in contemporary poetry.

Notes

1. Robert Sabatier, *Histoire de la Poésie Française*, vol. 3, *La Poésie du
Vingtième Siècle, Métamorphoses de la Modernité* (Paris: Albin Michel, 1988).

2. I regret the absence of Anne-Marie Albiach in this project. She is un-
doubtedly one of the most trenchant poets now writing in France, as well as a
gifted translator of American poetry. However, she neither wanted to answer
my questionnaire nor, out of loyalty to her American translators, wished me to
translate her texts, though I had previously done so in a New York-based maga-
zine, *New Observations*, in a special issue I edited and translated, *Ecriture: The
French Mind*, no. 54 (Jan.–Feb. 1988).

3. Gil Jouanard, *120 poètes français d'aujourd'hui* (Montpellier: Maison du
Livre des Ecrivains, 1992). Henri Deluy and Liliane Giraudon, *Poèsies en France
dupuis 1960: 29 Femmes Poétes, Une Anthologie* (Paris: Stock, 1994). For
other anthologies, see Jeanine Moulin, *Huit siècles de Poésie féminine, Anthologie,
1170–1975* (Paris: Seghers, 1981). For the twentieth century, she lists sixty-
seven women, not including the ones I have selected. Other presentations in-
clude Jean Rousselot, *Poètes français d'aujourd'hui* (Paris: Seghers, 1959), which

features only one woman, Claire Goll, out of sixty-one poets presented; Bernard Delvaille, *La Nouvelle poésie française, Anthologie* (Paris: Seghers, 1974), where, out of ninety-seven poets, there are three women: Adeline, Geneviève Clancy, and Françoise Thieck. A more modest effort is to be found in *La Nouvelle poésie féminine*, selected by Gisèle Halimi and Jean Breton, *Poésie* 1 (Jan.–Apr. 1975): 39–40. Here there are twenty-nine poets, excluding avant-garde poets such as Anne-Marie Albiach and Danielle Collobert. These poets, on the other hand, are to be found in Henri Deluy, *L'Anthologie arbitraire d'une nouvelle poésie, 1960–1982: trente poètes* (Paris: coll. "Poésie," Flammarion, 1983). He features Albiach, Collobert, Marie Etienne, Geneviève Huttin, and Jacqueline Risset. Lastly, and by the same anthologist, *Poésie en France, 1983–1988, une anthologie critique* (Paris: Flammarion, 1989). Out of fifty-eight poets, there are five women, including Albiach, Etienne, Michelle Grangaud, Josée Lapeyrère, and Esther Tellermann.

4. An early combative collection of this group's positions is found in *Tel quel, théorie d'ensemble* (Paris: coll. "Tel Quel," Editions du Seuil, 1968); among the contributors are Foucault, Barthes, Derrida, Kristeva, Risset, and Sollers. Three years prior to that publication and indicative of its linguistic orientation was *Théorie de la Littérature, textes des formalistes russes réunis*, selected and translated by Tzvetan Todorov, preface by Roman Jakobson (Paris: coll. "Tel Quel," Editions du Seuil, 1965). For a more personal note, see Jean Thibaudeau, *Mes Années Tel Quel* (Paris: Ecritures, 1994), 56–68, on the beginnings; on the political position, see 121–154. And, unquestionably, the most important publications on the subject are Philippe Forest, *Histoire de Tel Quel* (Paris: Editions du Seuil, 1995), and the double issue of *L'Infini* entitled "De Tel quel à l'Infini" (March 1995): 49–50.

5. See my introduction and translation of Joyce Mansour, *Cris/Screams* (Sausalito, CA: Post-Apollo Press, 1995).

6. These poets as well as other women poets figure prominently in the following French anthologies: *Vingt poètes américains*, edited and selected by Jacques Roubaud and Michel Deguy (Paris: NRF/Gallimard, 1980); *21 + 1 Poètes américains d'aujourd'hui*, selected by Emmanuel Hocquard and Claude Royet-Journoud (Montpellier: Delta, 1986); and again by the same two poets, *49 + 1 nouveaux poètes américains* (Royaumont: Un bureau sur l'Atlantique et Action poétique, 1991); and most recently, "Trois + un poètes américains," *Action poétique*, no. 137 (winter 1994–95). Here the poets are Norma Cole, Rosmarie Waldrop, and Laura Moriarty.

7. See my introduction in *Toward a New Poetics: Contemporary Writing in France* (Berkeley: University of California Press, 1994).

8. Oulipo can best be described as a mathematically defined game of verbal construction forcing the poet (e.g., Jacques Roubaud) or fiction writers (e.g., Georges Perec, Raymond Queneau) to adhere to the severest rules founded on

rhythmic, structural, and lexical preoccupations. See *Oulipo: la littérature potentielle* (Paris: Gallimard, 1971); *Oulipo: Atlas de littérature potentielle* (Paris: Gallimard, 1981); and *La bibliothèque oulipienne* (n.d.; reprint, Genève and Paris: Slatkine, 1981). For a recent evaluation, see Jean-Jacques Thomas, *La Langue la poésie, essai sur la poésie française contemporaine* (Lille: Presses Universitaires de Lille, 1989), esp. 163–86.

9. See n. 63 in my *Toward a New Poetics* for Zukofsky's status in France. See also my *Louis Zukofsky "A" (sections un à sept)*, notes and introduction by Serge Gavronsky, translated by Serge Gavronsky and François Dominique (Dijon: Ulysse fin de siècle, 1994).

10. Barthes stated that he preferred texts where the principle is that "the subject is but an effect of language." *Roland Barthes par Roland Barthes* (Paris: coll. "Ecrivains de toujours," Editions du Seuil, 1975), 82.

11. Jean-Christophe Bailly, *au-delà du langage, Une étude sur Benjamin Péret* (Paris: Eric Losfeld, 1971), 41.

12. Malcolm Bowie, "Solitary Muses, the Widening Gap between French and English Poetry," *Times Literary Supplement*, 27 January 1995, 11–12.

13. The emphasis on the void, on the text, on the questioning of language by itself, can most clearly be read in the poets gathered in Emmanuel Hocquard-Raquel, *Orange Export Ltd., 1969–1986* (Paris: coll. "Poésie," Flammarion, 1986). A more recent critique on poetry and politics is found in *Lignes* 16 (June 1992), with a contribution by Jacqueline Risset, "L'envers du tapis" (33–39). It is noteworthy that in this same issue there is an homage to Edmond Jabès who was particularly sensitive to the complex relationship between language, textuality, and the thematics of writing.

14. In an interview in *Le Monde*, 10 February 1995, 12, Valère Novarina, one of the most original dramatists and writers in recent years, provided yet another answer to the question of language, when he quoted Saint Augustine: "Language is heard but thought is seen."

15. Leslie Kaplan has also written "Cassavetes, Dostoievski et le meurtre," *Cahiers du cinéma* 451 (January 1992): 40–43, and "Children, children: depuis longtemps déjà nous ne naissons plus de pères vivants," *Trafic* 1 (winter 1991): 45–51.

16. Douglas Robinson, *The Translator's Turn* (Baltimore and London: Johns Hopkins University Press, 1991), pt. 2, "Dialogical Turns."

17. Michelle Grangaud, *Mémento-Fragments, Anagrammes* (Paris: P.O.L., 1987), and *Stations, Anagrammes* (Paris: P.O.L., 1990).

18. Jean Starobinski, *Les mots sous les mots, Les anagrammes de Ferdinand de Saussure, essai* (Paris: coll. "Le Chemin," NRF/Gallimard, 1971), see, e.g., 23–26. One might also consult "The Two Saussures" *Semiotext(e)* 1, no. 2 (fall 1974), which contains a text by Jean Starobinski as well as Saussure's own "Letter on the Anagrams."

19. Michelle Grangaud's "Rush," in *Poésies en France depuis 1960: 29 Femmes, Une Anthologie* (Paris: Stock, 1994), 87–97.

20. Joseph Guglielmi, *Origine de la mer* (Xanrupt and Longemer [Fr.]: Aencrages, 1993), unpaginated.

21. The trobairitz include such poets as Azalais de Porcairagues, Bieris de Romans, and, perhaps the best known, the Comtesse de Die. Texts are few; many are anonymous. The word itself is found in a thirteenth-century romance, *Flamenca*, where a woman writing poetry is called a *bona trobairis*. The root *trobar* (to invent, to compose) is joined to the suffix *-airitz*, sign of a feminine gender in opposition to the male suffix *-ador*. See William D. Peden, ed., *The Voice of the Trobairitz: Perspectives on the Women Troubadours* (Philadelphia: University of Pennsylvania Press, 1989), 13.

22. Anne Portugal, *Fichier* (Paris: Michel Chandeigne, 1992), 50.

23. Henri Deluy, *Marina Tsvetaieva: L'Offense lyrique* (Paris: Fourbis, 1992). See in particular the section bearing the name of the book, 16–18, where Deluy concludes rather surprisingly that "there is no writing of poetry without lyricism" (18). Henri Deluy is not alone in appreciating the poet's genius. In 1990, Véronique Lossly authored a *Marina Tsvetaieva* for the series "Poètes d'aujourd'hui" published by Seghers; Marina Belkina wrote on *Le destin tragique de Marina Tsvetaieva* (Paris: Albin Michel, 1992); *Marina Tsvetaieva, Poèmes* (Paris: Editions Librairie de Globe, 1993); and lastly, ten (thin) volumes of her writings were published by Clémence Hiver (Paris: 1993).

24. Henry Deluy, translations of Marina Tsvetaieva's poems in *If* 1, no. 1 (1993).

25. Deluy, *Marina Tsvetaieva: L'offense lyrique*, 13.

26. Henri Deluy and Liliane Giraudon, *Marina Tsvetaieva* (La Souterraine [Fr.]: La Main courante, 1992), 6.

27. The Rimbaud text was most recently quoted in Christian Prigent, *Etre moderne est-ce être illisible?* (Reims: Au Bar de la Comédie de Reims, 1992). As a polemical and highly provocative critic, I would also recommend his *Ceux qui MerdRent* (Paris: P.O.L., 1991), where he reviews some of the major poets of our time, including Char, Ponge, Perec, and Denis Roche as well as (and that is the reason for the capital *R*) Alfred Jarry. He also reviews the work of more recent writers such as Valère Novarina.

28. *Roland Barthes par Roland Barthes*, 51. Barthes returns to one of his favorite words throughout his autobiography, see, e.g., "Doxa/paradoxa," 75.

29. See Jacqueline Risset, interview by Catherine Strasser, *Interlope la curieuse*, 7–8 June 1993, 95.

30. See, e.g., Paul Zumthor, *Essai de poétique médiéval* (Paris: coll. "Poétique," Editions du Seuil, 1972), esp. chaps. 5–7.

31. Jacque Roubaud, *La Fleur inverse, l'art des troubadours*, 2d ed., rev. and exp. (Paris: Les Belles Lettres, 1994), 344.

32. See Marcelin Pleynet, *Rime* (Paris: coll. "Tel Quel," Editions du Seuil, 1981). One should not forget that Risset is also the author of *Marcelin Pleynet* (Paris: coll. "Poètes d'aujourd'hui," Seghers, 1988).

Six Contemporary French Women Poets

Leslie Kaplan
Photograph by John Foley

Leslie Kaplan

What is it, within the *interior of prose* that for me, poetically, maintains a highly demanding posture? Movement, rhythm, punctuation, *pause*. And—the silence *within* words.

And the essential notion of encounter (surprising, astonishing, an "openness"—but of an encounter): the real, all of the real, encountered.

The goal of poetics: something irreceivable, and that, nevertheless, must be figured. I will take as my example something uttered by Dostoyevsky's character Ivan Karamazov, who says: "I am not mad, I'm only an assassin." That is for me a phrase ("irreceivable" but . . .) that goes furthest toward a high poetic exigence. (And the proof? It stupefies. Is there anything else one can make of it?) Here is a second example, and just as perfect, taken from a book I have just reread, *The Madness of Day* [*De la folie du Jour*]: "But I am sure of the following astounding truth: I experience a limitless pleasure in living and I shall have, in dying, a limitless satisfaction." Irreceivable and yet in need of being defined: that's it.

Now as to being a woman, may I quote Proust? "I will construct my book, I dare not say ambitiously like a cathedral but, quite simply, like a dress."

Besides that, I like Blanchot, Dostoyevsky, psychoanalysis, Brecht's writings on the theater, and those of Serge Daney on film; lots of films: *The Night of the Hunter* by Cassavetes, and Buñuel who looked for "the unknown and the strange" in the

I

world of street kids (and: "I hope never to do anything unworthy or reassuring"), and Rossellini.

And a single theme or so it seems to me. Everything. Seriously. At every turn, everything. Or, to put it another way, how is it possible, every time, to resolve the contradiction between what one knows *and* what one discovers, the movement of it. (The question of themes is connected to a high poetic exigence and, for me, raises the question of *polyphony*.)

As far as women in poetry, I don't know.

As far as the end of the century is concerned, *Wozu*! [What for!] Poetry in these times of distress? The question remains on the cutting edge today.

ॐ

Leslie Kaplan was born in New York City in 1943. She now lives and writes in Paris. Among her publications are the following:

L'Excès-L'usine. Paris: P.O.L., 1982. 2d printing, 1987, with an interview by Marguerite Duras; 3d printing, 1993.
Le Livre des ciels. Paris: P.O.L., 1983.
Le Criminel. Paris: P.O.L., 1985. 2d printing, 1996.
Le Pont de Brooklyn. Paris: P.O.L., 1987. Reprint, Paris: Folio/Gallimard, 1991.
L'épreuve du passeur. Paris: P.O.L., 1988.
"Règne." *Théâtre Public* 84 (Nov.–Dec. 1988).
Le Silence du diable. Paris: P.O.L., 1989.
Les Mines de sel. Paris: P.O.L., 1993.
"Miss Nobody Knows." In *Poésies en France depuis 1960: 29 Femmes poètes, Une anthologie*, edited by Liliane Giraudon and Henri Deluy. Paris: Stock, 1994.
"Somebody Killed Something." In *Le Cinéma des écrivains*. Paris: Editions de Cahiers du cinéma, 1995.
Depuis maintenant. Paris: P.O.L., 1996.

She has translated, together with Claude Régy, Wallace Stevens's *Trois voyageurs regardent un lever de soleil* (Arles: Actes Sud/Papiers, 1988). Among her works that have been translated into English:

Extracts from *L'Excès-L'usine* and *Le Livre des ciels*. Translated by Cole Swenson.

In *Violence of the White Page: Contemporary French Poetry*, edited by Stacy Doris, Phillip Foss, and Emmanuel Hocquard. Special issue of *Tyuonyi*, nos. 9–10 (1991).

The Brooklyn Bridge. Translated by Thomas Spear. Barrytown, NY: Station Hill Press, 1992.

Extracts from *The Brooklyn Bridge*. Translated by Serge Gavronsky. In Serge Gavronsky, *Toward a New Poetics: Contemporary Writing in France*. Berkeley: University of California Press, 1994.

જ₀

The factory, the factory universe, the one
breathing for you. There's no other air but the one it
pumps, rejects.

One is on the inside.

All spaces are occupied: everything has become
garbage. Skin, teeth, eyes.

One moves around in between shapeless partitions. One
comes across people, sandwiches, coke bottles,
instruments, paper, crates, screws. One moves in a
vague manner, outside time. Neither beginning nor end.
Things exist together, simultaneously.

Inside the factory, things are being made all the time.

One is inside, in the great factory universe, the one
breathing for you.

(*L'Excès-L'usine*, 11)

The factory, one goes there. Everything is there.
One goes there.
The excess-the factory.

A wall in the sun. Extreme tension. Wall, wall, a
small grain, brick on brick, or the cement or often
white, a sickly white or the fissure, a little earth,
grayness. The wall, its volume. At the same time,
that sun. Life is, hatred and light. Life as an oven,
before the beginning, complete.

She is grabbed, she is turned around, she is inside.

The wall, the sun. One forgets everything.

Most of the women have a marvelous toothless grin.

They drink coffee near the coffee stand.

The yard, one's got to cross it.

Sit on a crate.

Tensions, forgetting.

(*L'Excès-L'usine,* 12)

Cables are made near the window. The cables have
lots of colors, they're coiled up in circuits. There's
light, the space gives. One comes, one goes.
Corridors, forgetting.

Cables are made near the window. Extreme tension. The
sky, and the cables, it's all shit. One is gripped,
pulled by the cables, the sky. There's nothing else.

All spaces are occupied: everything has become
garbage. The skin is lifeless. Teeth bite into an
apple, a sandwich. One absorbs, the eyes stick to
everything like flies.

One works nine hours, the machine punches holes into
the pieces. The piece is put in place, the lever
brought down, the piece removed, the lever raised.
There's paper everywhere.

Time is outside, in things.

(*L'Excès-L'usine*, 13)

The yard, one's got to cross it. Total nostalgia
for a factory yard.

One moves around in between shapeless partitions.
Sheet metal, giving and greasy. What's the point, what
is the point. That wire on the ground. Nobody knows
the misery I've seen. One goes looking. One absorbs
everything. One goes, one walks down. One sees the
others doing something. The woman is alone, she exists
in her gestures. One walks, one feels the walk. One
is inside. One feels each movement, one straightens
up, one walks.

One eats caramels, one's teeth stick together.

Before going in, one has a fast one at the bar. One
stares at oneself in the mirror above the counter. The
jukebox is always playing Those were the days, my love,
ah yes those were the days.

(*L'Excès-L'usine*, 14)

One parks the bike. The yard is full of rounded paving stones.

In the rear, platforms. The paving stones make up a special surface, calm.

One crosses the air. In between the stones, pointed tufts.

Nothing disappears, ever. The air swells up, at each moment, with smells.

One walks forward in the circular yard. Above, the sky, naive. One is afraid, all the time.

The women arrive in loose dresses. No problem, one sees their breasts.

The space is divided, it's aweful.
The women are not protected.

One comes, one goes. Springtime, cruel and giving.
Factory, the factory, first memory.

(L'Excès-L'usine, 70)

When one gets there, the frigidaire in a corner is
large and white.
A couple of wires around. Things hang.

There're appliances, hollow basins, a buffet.
The basins are blue and yellow.
One sits, one has a drink.

In front, the shelves. They stand out.
One dreams, always. The shelves have trimmings.

There's a porous consistency to the piece.
A silence. The women are seated.

Very present sense of space. Curved things. The wall
gives, a lot.

A calendar hangs for the days. Taken up again and
mended and always, walking through that same room.
Wires. One is there.

Things on the buffet. Useless things, it's aweful.

Ample spaces, colors. Pieces and things, rubber.
The piece keeps on sliding. One is inside.

(*L'Excès-L'usine*, 83)

It's evening. There's time.

A tranquil mood sets in. Things fall down, all of them.

There're pictures on the wall, glued and flattened out. Objects stand in isolation. Worries. Around, it's the tablecloth and the blanket, and the crocheted bedcover. The curtains, too, look very much like wool.

On the other side of the windows, the suburb, wide and spacious. One feels it. One is among friends, and you are appreciated, immobility.

The room is there, round. No one knows, no one. She gulps down her meal. She sits in a chair, her hands, her knees.

Something dies, what violence.

On the other side, somebody's face, withdrawn and supple like a part of the body.

(*L'Excès-L'usine*, 84)

I wait for him by the subway exit. It's night, the
sky wavers. People speak to each other.

He comes wearing a leather jacket, smoking a cigarette.
I look at him as he climbs up the steps. Violent
movement. Something opens and remains lost. Clear
sky, transparent.

We reach a small narrow square surrounded by street
lamps. On the corner there's an interior decorator's
shop, rolls of paper, accessories. On the walls, city
posters.

It's an evening moment, ambiguous and clear as a point.
Around, people, their doubts.

(*Le Livre des ciels*, 64)

He takes me to see his mother. She lives in the
suburbs.

It's a small two-storied house. The walls are painted
blue and pink. I sit down, the guest.

Spacious house, and fixed up, sewn up. Curtains
everywhere. The radio is on all the time.

We sleep in the large bed, upstairs. It's the family
bed. The mother sleeps downstairs.

Around, fields, brown potatoes. A couple of buildings,
spread out. I look at the children coming home.
Others remain, on the balconies.

(*Le Livre des ciels*, 65)

The small house, the room. I walk in.
Everybody's there. Walls and chairs, curtains.
It's compact, massive.

I eat. Names and verbs can move around.
Everybody's there, face against face.

The food is very good, very filling.
Bodies of animals gulped down, with vegetables.
Cream sauces, with milk.
Everybody's eating.

The walls are far away, far away. The radio is silent.
Nevertheless, one is enveloped. I smell the wallpaper.

Invisible wires for the decor, there are none.
There are eyes, and hatred, without object, tolerant.

(*Le Livre des ciels*, 72)

Nature is there, outside. One takes a walk.

In the corridors, within, odors move around.
They disperse, return. One can neither touch them, nor
see them.

Those large windows. Beyond, a huge green floral
display, blocks of wood. Sun, and white air, caught.
One looks. It's clear and confusing, pure, in a way.

The place is artificial, built up. One doesn't like
it.
One gets there by train, to see it.

Trees, a pond. People often throw things in it. A man
threw a machine in it, a sophisticated appliance with
wires.

There's a scattering of many small buildings.
House phones, liaisons.

One talks a lot, almost everybody does it. One finds
easy words.

("Règne," 99)

Fairs, with fireworks. A mix of people.

One eats enormously. Soup, meat, dessert.
The wine is good. Some don't eat anything at all.

For sleeping, there're rooms.
One see trees, from everywhere one sees them.

One gets there by train. Then a little further by car.
One is driven.

Details, very important little things.
One thinks of them.

The fact of getting there by train already creates,
without a doubt, a sense of detachment, of excitement.
Nothing is possible in a state of euphoria.

("Règne," 100)

There are passionate love affairs, often between
close friends. One pampers oneself, one has beautiful
hair. Teeth and skin are beautiful.

You sleep with whom you want. One dreams with the trees,
sometimes the wind. There's also the sky, like a film,
and its movement, its slight noise.

Some windows are white, others blue.
All the panes are quite clean.

Around, the countryside is striated. People go through
it on bikes, with packs. One sees them, from afar.

("Règne," 101)

One plans extraordinary things, masked balls,
one puts up new walls. It's true. The music, there,
is also catchy, spinning.

One knows the way, one knows it, one knows it.

There are separate offices. Severe. There are sunken
armchairs against the walls, and photographs above.

The telephone, quite a bother. The switchboard is
elsewhere, in a small porous house.

Animals: Master them. A man rides around on
horseback, very handsome, wearing an earring, his
little daughter on his knees.

When it's hot, one stretches hammocks from the trees.
There are often cats in the branches. Elsewhere,
mosquito bites, flies.

("Règne," 102)

The sheets, how to describe them? They envelop the beds. One slips inside, one sleeps. But one keeps on hearing steps on the stairs and knocking on doors.

One strolls about, calmly. Above, the ceilings with their curves.

The toilets are often clogged up, disagreeable. Otherwise, large rooms, long and narrow, with pipes climbing up, lively colors.

In the morning, a big breakfast, very nourishing, which lasts, with comings and goings. In the middle of the room, a stately coffee machine, its shiny dials.

("Règne," 103)

Before leaving there's always a get-together. The people are there, in their chairs, light-hearted. One takes one's time, one discusses freely.

The words, of course, are given.

Young old words, available, where one can rest and wait.

("Règne," 104)

Michelle Grangaud

Photograph by John Foley

Michelle Grangaud

It is not easy to speak about oneself, at least correctly. It is not easy for me to speak about my writing. When I think about it, it all appears commonplace, anecdotal, futile. Others know how to speak correctly about writing and about their own writing. When I say "correctly," I mean placing oneself at a certain distance from oneself, neither too close nor too far away. In my case it is with a degree of awkwardness that I situate myself.

In relationship to writing, all the more awkward because I do not dispose of any theoretical or critical apparatus of my own that would allow me to situate myself. Everything is chance, everything occurs blow by blow. And at the present time, I find myself very divided. The fact that my first three published books [*Mémento-Fragments*, *Stations-Anagrammes*, and *Renaîtres*] are anagrammatic collections is the result of a personal accident and not at all the fruit of a penchant for writing under constraints.

Perhaps here anagrams should be defined: transposition of the letters of a word or of a group of words in such a way as to form other words, neither losing nor adding any letters. It is a constraint reputed difficult, but in fact, no more so than scrabble or crossword puzzles. And, rather than a constraint, I have always felt it to be a technique. Once acquired, it becomes a working tool. Question of meaning: constraint fixes attention on phonemes and, as a result, masks meaning, reality. Out of my anagrammatic practice emerges, nevertheless, fragments of reality, often the most violent, that surface independently of all desire to speak. This involuntary return of reality transforms, so it seems to me, the anagram into something other than a pure exercise in virtuosity. One can say as much about all forms of poetic writing. There is a division, the intentionality of discourse (and of a personal affectivity) that find themselves short-circuited, and as of that, the anecdotal falls to the side.

I call anecdotal the whole process of identification, beginning with the problem of proper names. It seems to me that being forced to carry a name, for a writer or a poet, and what is more, a *proper* name, constitutes a serious contradiction. When the question is asked, insofar as I am concerned, I think of a pseudonym, as so many others have doubtlessly done before, but this makes matters worse, a sort of narcissistic emphasis. Now I regret not having thought of taking for a name my social security number or rather, since it is a bit too long to say out loud, the last three digits, which I prefer because they are the most insignificant ones, or the two key digits: zero-four would then appear to me to be a relatively acceptable name.

It seems to me that it is always the greatest absence of identity that produces the most powerful singularity in the case of a writer or a poet. In order to be original, begin by copying—that's what Proust says. And singularity, as a criterion of aesthetic value, is so readily received that one should not insist on this.

In my childhood, what most contributed to the shaping of my thought, what nourished my appetite for reading and writing, were myths: *The Odyssey, Thousand and One Nights,* and the Bible, which I read not out of a religious conviction but out of a taste for myth. I knew very early on that Bible meant *Book.* And for a long time I remained persuaded that the first sentence in Genesis was: "In the beginning was the Word, and the Word was with God, and the Word was God." In fact, that is the first verse in the Gospel according to John. I long marveled at that sentence. That said, my love of myths is inversely proportional to the one I have for religions in general and to Christian variants in particular.

Direct influences on my current work: William Burroughs for cutups and Unica Zürn in whom I discovered the possibility of the anagrammatic poem. Finally, with the American objectivist poets, I found a manner of theorizing, a way of writing that I had already begun to practice intuitively, that is, in a less-than-rigorous manner. There is no doubt that it was not by chance that I found my sources in languages other than French. At one time, Proust influenced me, and markedly so, as much in my ways of thinking as in my writing. He held sway over me to such an extent, fascinated me so, that I finally realized that I had to turn away from him, to separate myself from him.

Philosophy (Spinoza in the first place), psychoanalysis, films (but I have not seen one for many years), contemporary painting and music—all the forms of a pure consumption. But in general I do not feel any influence at all, other than very indirect, on my ways of writing.

I would like to practice writing prose again, the litheness, the fluidity of prose, all the while holding on to the anagrammatic lesson of a nonintentional discourse and, this goes without saying, without an identity.

Does the fact of being a woman play a role in my thinking? Without a doubt, without a doubt it plays a part, but what part I would not be able to say. It truly conceals its role. In fact, I have a tendency of suspecting it, this being-woman; it appears to me to be a bit like a false brother. The dictionary tells us that the term poetess quickly acquired a pejorative connotation. That is a societal truth, probably more so in a Mediterranean society, a fact that, unfortunately, does not affect only poetesses! In painting, music sculpture, architecture—the feminine quote simply does not exist. No need to discuss it. And yet we have in the government a minister for women to defend us; we—we are also battered wives, daughters raped by their fathers and secretaries by their bosses in that sweet land of France with its legendary gallantry. There is much bread on the table for our minister for women, but it seems we are not eating our share of it.

Poetry, as we near the end of the century, of course, is in a state of confusion. Perhaps less induced by what is explicitly denounced (the crisis in publishing, increasing popularity of television's ineptitude) than by a historical and political questioning. On the one hand, we possess an enormous cultural stockpile. It is difficult, in front of such a mountain of masterpieces, not to feel one's individual insignificance. On the other hand, the question has always been asked, but it seems to me that today it is asked with redoubled acuity: artistic activity, in its demands for singularity (from which it distinguishes itself from other aesthetic activities in general—artisanal, folkloric—or the techniques of mass production), is it anything other than a healthy, well-fed activity? What if only the well fed had access to a privileged condition on this earth where, to a large extent, famine reigns and all around there's extreme poverty? I certainly do not believe I have an answer to this double question; simply, it happens that, at times, I ask it of myself.

❧

Michelle Grangaud was born in 1941 in Algiers and now lives and works in Paris. Her publications include:

Mémento-Fragments, Anagrammes. Paris: P.O.L., 1987.
Renaîtres. Paris: Ecbolade, 1990.
Stations, Anagrammes. Paris: P.O.L., 1990.
Geste, Narrations. Paris: P.O.L., 1991.
Jours le Jour, chronique. Paris: P.O.L., 1994.

Her work has appeared in *Action poétique, Banana Split, Détail, Lendemains* (Berlin). Her work in progress as well as published texts were discussed by Christian Rosset on the French radio program *France-Culture*, 8 December 1991.

A version of the texts included here and translated by Serge Gavronsky appeared in *TriQuarterly* 94 (fall 1995).

❧

The waiting room
is totally empty.
Oddly enough, the chairs are very present.

When the alarm rings
he stretches out his arm,
pushes the button before opening his eyes.

The sign says:
it is forbidden
to walk on the tracks. Danger of death.

Thunder grumbles,
red-glowing embers,
only half a cigarette remains.

They live above,
they live below,
they meet at crossings without seeing one another.

The train is about to leave,
he runs down the platform
mumbling incomprehensible words.

She hangs the laundry
on the line.
The sheets smack in flight toward a windy sky.

The bird flutters its wings,
it does not move,
it stays aloft, still, and flutters its wings.

Tired out and sweaty.
Punctured eardrums,
palms press the drill down.

It will be a beautiful day,
we shall go to the woods
full of plastic bags and wax paper.

Sitting on a bench,
legs spread out,
he looks at the ground between his shoes.

An hour left
before school's out.
She turns to look at the window.

The travel bag
weighs on his shoulder,
inside, shoes and books.

She no longer knows
what's the day. It
seems to her today's a Thursday.

A need to love
just a vague desire.
Wishing to rub against another body.

Classes for beginners.
Handicapped
from foreign countries.

The lake in the dream
was smooth and white.
An obscure threat troubled the deep.

Distant horizon
of this flat countryside.
Hushed voices behind the wall.

House in the suburbs,
they've bought it,
between buildings and vacant lots.

It's raining. It rained.
It shall rain. He walks,
head low, passerby under the rain.

To do the housework is
To wipe everything clean:
grease, traces, the idea of death.

They take the bus
to go downtown.
Smell of rubber and sighing doors.

She cuts the
pear in thick slices,
poaches them in sugary water.

They were many
to celebrate:
their team had won the European Cup.

The siren shrieks.
It's an ambulance.
In the traffic jam somebody's going to die.

The leaves on the trees
flutter. The wind
rushes up in the air with a paper.

She leans
against the back
of the armchair, eyes closed, thumb in her mouth.

He cries out, be careful.
But it's too late. The child's
already been hit by a van.

Corn on the cob
roasts on
the grill. There's a very sweet smell rising up.

Sitting on the ground,
she holds out her hand,
her young daughter asleep across her lap.

He bends over
to tie his laces.
His fingers tremble a lot and his vision blurs.

She wears a straw hat
with a somber
blue ribbon, it's a souvenir.

A chilly early morning,
the water in the kettle
always seems to start trembling.

In front of the sink,
standing, quickly
swallowing antidepressants.

Earplugs
out of the machine:
pull the handle, they drop into your hand.

He goes to check in
at the unemployment office,
from having smoked so much, his heart is beating.

She no longer
wants to open the shutters,
no longer wants to leave, no longer wants light.

He writes: you know.
Then puts the pen down
to think. Lights a cigarette.

She dips the
tips of her fingers in water
to feel them ringed.

The population
is indicated on
the map in different-size circles.

A tear pearls
between the eyelids,
swells then slides down the length of her cheek.

Slip and brassiere
are soaked in
soapy water with iridescent bubbles.

Turning their backs
they undress,
naked they fall, roll one toward the other.

She opens the door,
walks into the room,
turns on the light, sees them naked.

On the graveled
shoulder of
the road, there's the cat, head crushed.

She sees herself
in the mirror.
Circles under her eyes and pale.

Twisted leaves
slip across tombstones
and fly past the feet of passersby.

Must get up,
must shake
this fat sack of flesh and those stiff bones.

He holds the match,
offers her the flame,
caresses her cheek with the tips of his fingers.

She left without
looking back toward
what she was leaving, didn't want to cry.

The fly on the pane,
its feet quiver.
Its snout emerges and sucks on God knows what.

The picture is taken
on the beach. They
formed a pyramid. They're all laughing.

She says to herself she'll
never get there
on time for her appointment. He never waits.

Water hose on
the fence,
posters: flying pieces of paper.

One two three and four,
five, six, seven, eight, nine
ten—eleven, that's too much for a child's hand.

It's morning. In
all the offices, people
greet each other in a friendly way.

With the tip of his nail, he
tries to extract
a piece of steak stuck in his teeth.

She rips off
his glasses, throwing
them out the open window into the street.

He didn't understand
what had happened:
suddenly the plate lay on the floor in pieces.

She shades her
eyes with her hand
and walks down the sunlit corridor.

The days are long,
it's summer. Flashes
of thunder in the stifling night.

Tips of breasts. They are
gray in the shadow of
the room, lit only by a streetlamp.

He sees himself in a dream
following an unknown woman.
She hobbles, one heel higher than the other.

She turns off the lamp.
Lies down and thinks again
about what she'll put down in her will.

Kites by
the hundreds. The child
sees the sky like a roof trembling with colors.

She's alone in a bus,
someone vomited.
One sees the sun under the puddles.

He unbuttons his fly,
pisses a long time
on the corrugated sheet-metal fence.

Loud laughter,
sharp as a cry,
the squeal of an animal caught in a trap.

The sharp smack,
just after the lightning:
the neighborhood suddenly plunged in darkness.

Pavillons-sous-Bois,
Fontenay-sous-Bois,
Aulnay, Clichy, Rosny, nothing but concrete.

Feet,
crowds of feet,
ceaselessly stamping on the sidewalk.

He holds a pencil,
sticks his tongue out
draws a hanged man sticking out his tongue.

As she throws the living
crab into the boiling water,
she catches sight of the child's terrified look.

In the barracks.
He waits his turn,
waits to take a shower. Bored.

Adult education
programs
in public-school buildings.

Adenoma of the liver,
the doctor says.
Is that enough to stop you from having another drink?

Between thumb and
index, she curls,
nervous fingers, a strand of her hair.

He slips his hand,
furtively, under the table.
Under her skirt, feels her very soft skin, naked.

On the computer
keyboard, she
types in: departure 9:35.

Enormous machine
reducing the gesture
to a solitary movement of ghostly fingers.

The shadow of the room
striated by slits
in the shutters. Lighter rays of light.

He shaves. Wonders
how he'll be able
to tell her, he no longer wants her.

She says, Johnny,
with a smile,
Johnny, you know, he was all my youth.

The nurse wheels
her rolling bed
toward the delivery room for the birth.

She holds the peach
under the faucet,
tastes, under the water, its velvety skin.

The child is slapped,
traces of fingers,
a volley, marking her temples.

The light is off,
she twists around
in bed, can't get to sleep.

It's 2 A.M.
He walks alone
up the boulevard. Not even a cat on the sidewalks.

Rain on windows
leaves traces.
You'd say they were tears held back.

After a day
of work, you've got
to do the shopping for the evening meal.

He seals the door
and the windows with
tape before turning on the gas.

An accident,
2 dead and 6
seriously injured on Interstate 13.

The air is transparent.
The weather will change.
They say one doesn't know what to wear anymore.

Her arm reaches out
of the toll booth
gives all those vacationers their change.

He looks over
his paycheck.
Checks out everything on his calculator.

One's got to repeat
the same work,
pearling it off, thirty-nine hours per week.

One goes to the beach,
naked feet in the sand,
and smells the scent of suntan lotion.

The Down-syndrome child
splashes his
bathwater all around and laughs.

He takes his cat
in his arms, brings him
to the vet to be fixed.

The sirens whistle,
it's already noon,
first Wednesday of the month. She sighs.

His eardrums
shudder to
the noise of machines. Hello deaf-mute.

A pain in the right breast.
And that lump.
Go see a doctor. Can't. Too afraid.

He's cold,
huddled up
on the ground, warming his hand between his thighs.

The mother explains
to her daughter the
plans she's made for the family vault.

We tried
to make love
in the tub. Hard and noisy.

Together they drank
water out of the tap.
Their lips grazed, their eyes laughed.

She threw back
her head. It was that
pleasure, pleasure without words, that pleasure.

The sea was calm,
he knew how to swim.
Difficult to know how he drowned.

She leans forward,
elbow on
the counter, and rests her forehead in her hand.

Seven A.M.
The train, in fifteen minutes.
He swallows his last gulp of sleep.

Greetings can be
contagious. On certain
mornings, they're positively epidemic.

At the store
he picks up an apple,
a banana, and a sprig of mint.

(*Geste, Narrations,* 7–20)

Anne Portugal

Photograph by Samson Portugal

Anne Portugal

THE GARDEN

> I believe in the world as I do in a daisy,
> because I see it, but I don't think about it.
> —Fernando Pessoa, *The Shepherd*

> I dream Verlaine translated Marina.
> —Liliane Giraudon, Preface,
> *Marina Tsvetaieva*, trans.
> Henri Deluy and Liliane Giraudon

> the gardener knows
> how to divide my time
> to move ahead
> each step folly in that step
> which I do not have to place
> there and which knows the end of the road
> —Anne Portugal,
> *De quoi faire un mur*

It's obvious. Floral displays are only for kindergarten teachers and window boxes. Let me stick with the gardener. How can I sum up the way I write poetry: Short and massive, line divisions, rectilinear alleys, pruning shears of laughter, and the impossibility of thinking about prose.

Or how to indicate to the other, in the most effective manner, what might be considered on the order of one's breathing, of one's own vital disorder. Or how to reduce—or to restore—a savage luxuriance to the powerful geometry of a poetic space that is the urban site of our encounters.

People are passing by, but they do not speak; poems pass by, but they do not think, unburdened (what a joy!) of the need to reach an opinion. They have the fugitive state of leaves, of fountains, of the dazzle of lights, or of the extreme nudity of winter. They are among others. They are the others. In the public domain, wrote Desnos.

Or the public garden as a privileged space of passing through and especially from the private to the public; where to show oneself, to expose oneself, is not directed at the collectivity but to a state of anonymity. Or rather, to be sure that in reading oneself, the other recognizes himself, as self, in the greatest indifference.

Since this garden is a place of assembly, it is also a space for vigilance. Against oneself, first of all, against the banalities of one's pitiful "excellence." And then, against that highway consensus— especially that one, as we near the end of the century, which would finally wish poetry to come back, under the pretext that the following would be recuperated: meaning, readability, religious aspirations, all of that in a bleached language, coded, in short, reappropriated. In that case, it is a question of keeping watch, that is to say, working on the razor's edge and caressing the blade. Which is a way of loving and laughing with an ax. Being a woman has nothing and everything to do with this. And to insist on our presence in anthologies, to insist on quotas, is a joke that turns us away from poetry and brings us back to institutional concerns. But who cares!

Let us rally round Emily Dickinson. We shall not save anything. We cannot pretend to any triumph, but we shall keep watch. "Love," she says, "precedes life and lives after death." We shall keep watch in a garden, and we shall fall asleep, of course, at the crucial moment. Poetry without illusion, after Gethsemane, as one says "after" a painter or in the "wake" of an event, accomplished, irretrievable. A way of writing poetry in order to know more about nothing.

No, poetry has not come back, neither is it on its way back. In the 1970s in France, it was marked by a violent exigence, in the grips of what many would like to call "a glacial period," provoked by the so-called excessive rigor of theoreticians. It is true that my elders shaped me in an iron corset, which did not really correspond to my rather baroque disposition, almost kitschlike. But I cared for that form of intense, exaggerated, surveillance that one imposed upon oneself in order to rid oneself of the problem of meaning, at least of its illusion. *De quoi faire un mur* [*Materials for a Wall*], as the title indicates, was the very result of that demanding attitude that I borrowed from Mondrian and that allowed me to manifest maximum emotions in terms of pure abstraction, through principles of horizontality and verticality, in brief, of a geometry of space. That was again the project in *Le plus simple appareil* [*The Simplest Apparel*] in which the rounded forms of the biblical Susanna, a painter's inspiration, which she exposed (danger) in a generous fashion, must be expressed by its equation of a spatial resolution in poetry, degreased by way of a secret without mystery, through laughter: "Keep moving! There's nothing to see."

If you wish, similar to the metaphysical rectitude of Reverdy's poems or a painting by Hopper: women look out a window, but we do not know what they see. Poetry might consist in aiming at something beyond a frame (the marvel of a window that outlines or a poetic verse that lines out), above emptiness, and that would allow one to gently cross over suspension bridges without being dizzy, even wearing heavy wooden clogs. An imaginary perfection obtained through imperfection itself, an extreme (Dominique Fourcade would call it "exstream") watched over by form. Not a question of turning one's back on the real but an effort to discover the formula of a motionless state, pulled along by a gardener's line. A disposition placed at a halfway point, mid-August. But nothing final, nothing sublime.

For that, my models have always been painters, for they are the ones who expose, within a fixed vision, a proposition and its resolution; and because I cannot think this through, this disappearance of space, I turn to them and they can make me see it.

For that, one would have to train lightheartedly and track down the serious. Let no one take poetry for . . . Let no poet take himself for . . . Equalize objects of the real and dissolve concrete experience in abstract and delicate speculation, through an impulsive phenomenon that would relieve us of existence and suspend us in the air.

For that, women-poets have always been dynamiters, Tsvetayeva or Gertrude Stein, for it is a question of bringing poetry back before the public, holding a "rod" to its back—so that it holds itself erect; so that it feels the weight of the world and its affects; that it feels its vertebrae, including its own death. Of a rebellious humor, a fighter and wild, one should play at taking hostages and let (all) the world tremble that it has nothing to give in exchange.

For that, the poets in this garden, all of them, are kind men, "the meek members of the Resurrection," Emily would say; the Verlaine of "La bonne chanson," the Shakespeare of *A Midsummer's Night's Dream* or of the sonnets, all of Ronsard, all of Apollinaire. What I gather from them, on the contrary, is their incredible mode of dissolving drama into melancholia or irony. What saves them is that curvature of the spine, concealed in the hollow of their texts, that suppleness that, at the very moment it reveals their mastery, abandons itself to a sensual language, even a daring one, even a facile one. French music, at the end of the nineteenth century, with Debussy or Ravel, found that very point of impact, inebriated by a suave elasticity, in the power of the mute *e*. Here is a possible connection, if there is one, between masculine and feminine in poetry, in a symmetrically inverse position. And given this, we work exactly at the same point of emotion—a question of rhythm, where we tighten it, where we let go. "The thing is slight, like all fecundation," writes Jude Stefan. Let things appear in order to be annulled, show them and, just as soon, erase them.

"That gathers a crowd
    the fragility of an aluminum armature
       which goes through blue
           carnations."

ॐ

Anne Portugal was born in 1949 in Angers, Maine-et-Loire, France. She is an *Agrégée de lettres modernes* and now lives and works in Paris. Among her publications are the following:

La Licence, Qu'on appelle autrement Parrhésie. Paris: Gallimard, 1980.
Les Commodités d'une banquette. Paris: P.O.L., 1985.
De quoi faire un mur. Paris: P.O.L., 1987.
Fichier. Paris: Editions Michel Chandeigne, 1992.
Le plus simple appareil. Paris: P.O.L., 1992.

Her work has appeared in *Po&Sie*, *Banana Split*, *Action poétique*, *Pandora's Box*, *Plurielle*, *Doc(k)s*, *La nouvelle revue de psychanalyse*, *Eclat*, and *Révolution*, as well as in the newspapers *Le Monde* and *L'Humanité*. Works that have been translated into English:

"Six Poems." Translated by Norma Cole. In *Violence of the White Page: Contemporary French Poetry*, edited by Stacy Doris, Phillip Foss, and Emmanuel Hocquard. Special issue of *Tyuonyi*, nos. 9–10 (1991).
"Four Poems." Translated by Norma Cole. In *Série d'écriture* 4. Providence, RI: Burning Deck, 1993.
Nude. Translated by Norma Cole. Los Angeles: Sun & Moon, 1997.

ॐ

You really know your art you
the right distance
moving back
the cat's eye in the marble factory
the flower pot with flowers
quite powerful
the red of the red bean
you'd need a rich uncle from the States even dead
even ugly
the hereditary symmetry of the rodeo
and its furious envy
to make your skittles dance
while whistling
think think of the guy from Falaise
and who relaxes
and who shoves you around
you really know your art you

(*Le plus simple appareil*, 9)

THE BATH

it's better to know her name
to lay out the scene
with her name
it gives out on a meadow

the value of an oath
at the level of the green
and an approximation of ease
and charity

(*Le plus simple appareil*, 13)

my Susanna
is violet I think
and heavyset
weighty no her given name
in Sweden would be
violent

I placed a heavyset woman
in Bayeux
under the Tree of Liberty
the blue spaces between the branches
drew the heads of two old men

(*Le plus simple appareil,* 14)

she who would take a bath
turning her back to the scene
not knowing what
she was getting into then I would tell her
that here the two old men would be
frozen really dried out and their
eyes too wouldn't be able
to sparkle even though ice
gets right to the bones of the old men

Susanna this landscape goes well with blondes

(*Le plus simple appareil,* 15)

because a ship
the bathtub
can just please
my Susanna
there's got to be water in it
rain
from elsewhere

(it's in the middle of a meadow)

first activity
the spoon
a similar shape
the cradle
would you want Alice to
no Sigourney Weaver
the day was breaking
and then those two assholes

                            (*Le plus simple appareil*, 16)

                    no curtain
                    no curtain

move move   the film credits

                  made by the compressor
          and the unwinding moving forward
                  and we who feel it
                    and the tar
                        pail
                    to the rear
                    to the rear

              set your bathtub there
                at the very place
          where the landing strip will be

                    (*Le plus simple appareil*, 17)

and don't you budge the skin hasn't settled
a sob a wrinkle
Susanna in her bath
only the title keeps you
twice over
from becoming an old man + an old man
you blush that's a fact
you increase the circulation under the skin
of the speed
of a wren
the distance from your heart to your cheeks
must go through a famous overcoat
rather cheap to buy by the square meter
for it's water out of the bath

(*Le plus simple appareil*, 18)

in return can't you see that the only
piece of blue
is never seen
why not place
a luggage rack on the edge
of the tub
paint your toenails
only concentrating
on inward
modesty
no we're not dead
can't you see
and if we blush
that's life
groping along

(*Le plus simple appareil*, 19)

Susanna is drenched
in a Normandie meadow I think
she's reigning and naked
like a blossoming apple tree

why so many friendly signs
I've stepped on a mine
Susanna
I haven't stopped anything
at all costs one must stop
the extravagant option of the slippers
and especially the satin
bathrobe

(*Le plus simple appareil*, 20)

and who really cares about the temperature
all poems are cold
on the ship-factory

Susanna too is only warmed
because she's naked
remember the "Placard Affair"
where we go back to a prohibition
to a fur coat
the king fisher's armor

Susanna is really only warmed
because they're old
and they act out
the tale of the ox and the donkey

(*Le plus simple appareil*, 21)

but in your place

a black woman
for sure
would do the trick
would air out
this convex
freezer
on the eyes
holding on to an
eyelash
(but the visitors
get in the way)
the vitrification
object B 12 delicately placed
don't run don't place your hand
below your heart
paper flower
23rd parallel
and me a fat pumpkin didn't
understand a thing about
Gauguin

The strongest model
if she leans over
if she makes a move
who'll speak about her arms raised and the fall
of bracelets all aligned in the flat countryside
but which isn't France

(*Le plus simple appareil*, 22–23)

ah! it's chic to be the Dauphin
that gets you to raise a queen's
ship in no time at all
the same goes for your tub
the feet which precipitate
upward that mass
shall cover over waves
like hair
of the Diones (her mother)
of those homoloseamonsters with heady heads
you'll often come back

it's a ship carried aloft by multiple waves

(*Le plus simple appareil,* 24)

a day at a country fair
apiarists move about
    like astronauts
a kiss for the queen costly costly
a stretch of dry bodies

gold-trimmed ribbon medal
there's Susanna bored offering
    with a dry heart

one would only need a house pet
to strike the set
the zzzzzzz running through one's fingers
black water
the tune of a zipper in olden times

(Le plus simple appareil, 25)

As she was lighting up her cigarette
it so happened
that the largest ashtray she found was the tub

a young man drawing up the plans
fitted her type
there were three of them

and she threw away cigarette and smoke
flinging them out together
and laughed instead

her waistline like a potter's wheel
can be tightened
even the object on a maritime horizon disappears

only a chance to get to know
like the others
just how sweet is a plot of land

(*Le plus simple appareil,* 26)

Josée Lapeyrère

Photograph by Alain Viner

Josée Lapeyrère

If influences or, rather, encounters have always given a new direction to both my life and my work, it may be because they have disturbed established ideas about line breaks, the lightning of the line, sudden breaches, breathing . . .

At the age of seventeen, I had a decisive encounter with André Breton's text "Il y aura une fois." At that time, I knew next to nothing about André Breton, but as of that day, I realized the incredible debt I owed him, since seconds after having read his poem, I started writing down my first and totally unexpected line of poetry.

A little later, as a medical student, I attended a psychoanalytical consultation at a hospital. That was an overwhelming encounter for me, since it suggested psychoanalysis as a completely new way of listening and interpreting.

At every turn, then, I had the impression of bringing to light a space to which I could accede, a language space, neither given nor guaranteed, but which I had to try to reach at all costs.

This bringing to light of that space seems to me to be as much a project for poetry as it is for psychoanalysis, even though the two work through distinctive practices. And yet both are resolutely linguistic and not at all psychological; both explicitly listen to sound and rhythm, linguistic equivocation, breaks in the line, caesuras, scansions, that is to say, the effective dimension of time in language, and both question meaning in a radical manner.

There were many other such encounters, for example, with the Chilean poet Godo Iommi, founder of "La Phalène"; with the painter Arden Quin, founder of the MADI movement; and with S. W. Hayter who, in his Atelier 17, taught me how to appreciate the consequences of the first tracings of a contingent line.

These three artists had in common a rigor and a lightness, the ability to accept the random and the accidental, as well as a great sense of humor. I owe them a lot.

E. E. Cummings, too, and the art of cutting up a line and bringing it back to the letter out of which an intense emotion emerges. And Basho, Dickinson, Apollinaire, Gertrude Stein, the Elizabethans, Mallarmé, etc., and La Fontaine, Bossuet, and Chateaubriand, and . . . and what happens to me everyday when I read my contemporaries (with whom I discuss such questions), and lovers, friends, bereavements, arguments, neighbors, time, adversaries, bicycle racing, and your questions.

I know neither what characterizes my writing nor what might be considered my principal themes. I only know that a poetic text insists on a perfect "detachment" from its author and that that condition is solely founded upon line breaks—the breaking up of lines being the very object of the workings of the poem.

It is not at all a question of a poem being "clear" or "transparent"; on the contrary, the poem owes it to itself to keep such questions open, maintaining complexity and paradox and, in that manner, assuring the inexhaustible fruition of the capital of language. And for that, the poem owes it to itself to be "cut up," not according to a linear structure of breaks, as in a statement, but according to what might be considered a torsion (as in a Möbius line).

At bottom, this means one would have to *change addresses* during the writing of a poem: letting go the old "I," the clichés, side glances, conventions, the ideal of friendly addresses, the ones we care for the most, and arrive at a moment when the poem seems to address itself to the *first comer*, to anyone, absolutely anyone, and not in banalizing itself, simplifying itself, "vulgarizing" itself, but by the simple tracing of a line, by a stroke and the cutting up of the line that would, as a result, allow a vacillating trail to remain open, always.

This, of course, does not occur without the presence of "symptoms" that intrigue, surprise, alert; without that particular trait that surely concerns to the maximum the one who writes and that, as we know it, constitutes our true access to the universal.

The satisfaction and the pleasure that the poem would then provide us would be double and fused: the pleasure of having traversed the thickness of language, its sonorous and rhythmic strata; *and* the pleasure of the "unexpected," the surprise in the surging forth of an unexpected meaning; but also the pleasure of meeting up once again with something concealed, something we had forgotten we knew.

All that is necessary, or else one falls either into "beautiful poetry"—perfectly boring—or into publicity slogans.

I find the practice of poetry very salubrious because it raises the question of meaning in a radical manner and in the correct way: one knows that a word can easily come and substitute itself for another word as long as its rhythmic and sonorous weight feels right. In this manner, the meaning of a poem changes radically. This substitution, which is current practice in the writing of poetry, affirms that poetic writing—without avoiding meaning—places into evidence the nonsense supported by either a sound or a letter or aleatory associations and their regroupings.

One also knows that the forward motion of a poem is sustained by these sonorous interlacings that belong to the logic of the signifier rather than to the overbearing, even killing, one of the chain of meaning.

And then, for me, fundamentally, there's always the hope that a rigorous and audacious poetic practice might result in disengaging us, however slightly, from our state of congenital stupidity, our beliefs, our old scenarios, and that all these antiquated habits would then be changed into a pure material through the working out of fragmentation and sonorous and rhythmic dissolution, thereby blocking the way to a stultified meaning.

Despite everything, we must entertain this hope. That's the reason a group of friends and I have decided to found a new magazine, *Zoom-Zoum*.

Outside of love scenes of all kinds, as well as imaginary ones, i.e., directly linked to the presence or the evocation of a man, the feeling of being a woman plays a rather small part in my thinking, or so it seems to me.

If few women are represented in poetry anthologies, it may be because, up to now, rather few women have taken the risk of being published. This appears to be changing.

It seems to me that in order to be read and acknowledged, the quality of the work counts more than gender. I have not found, except in rare and insignificant instances, what one might consider so-called sexist positions in my own writing. As the end of the century approaches, everything has changed and nothing has changed.

Poets are not exempt from poetic service—the cutting up of lines; working on meaning, on the half-said, etc.; exercising language.

But the canons of poetic beauty have changed: beautiful images, beautiful metaphors—what once was called "great poetry"—no longer have an easy life; their walls are tumbling down. Between the way of the descriptive statement, journalistic or policelike, the one founded on a linear breaking up of lines, which does not carry it off, and the way of beautiful, purring images, or again the ones founded on the attraction of generalization or the appeal of the void, one must find another way, other ways. Besides, the way is open—one only has to open it, and life continues.

&

Josée Lapeyrère is a doctor and practices psychoanalysis in Paris. Among her publications are the following:

Là est ici. Paris: "Poésie 2," Gallimard, 1978.
La Quinze chevaux. Paris: coll. "Poésie," Flammarion, 1987.
La 15 CV. Paris: Séguier, 1989.
Comment faire le tour, éloge de la course. Paris: Point Hors Ligne, 1992.
Belles joues les géraniums. Paris: Flammarion, 1994.

She is the founder of the magazine *Le temps des loups* and was associated with the La Phalène movement, founded by the Chilean poet Godo Iommi. In 1993, along with other poets, she founded *Zoom-Zoum*, a magazine of poetic games and exercises.

Her work has appeared in *Banana Split, Po&Sie, Action poétique, Ailleurs, In'hui, Doc(k)s, Siècles, Les Lettres françaises, Lingo, Diaria de Poesia*. She is at present poetry editor of *Le Discours psychanalytique*, and, until it folded, she was the poetry editor of the newspaper *Matin*.

As an artist, she has created transparent books—serigraphic weavings of letters, words, and poems on plexiglass. She has participated in numerous group shows at Beaubourg, Galerie C. Corre, Galerie NRA, as well as galleries in Italy and Japan and, with Madi, an international group founded by Arden Quin, in France, Italy, Argentina, New Mexico, and Spain.

෴

THE SKIRT

not

       the nude   but
              the clothing
which streams

down the back   in torrents
too lively   a green   streams
softened   on the buttocks
smooth flowing air spreading

      between the thighs   and

the silk

      there breathes

          in harmony   a
     woman   passing
ecstasy   and   pigeons

            (*La Quinze chevaux*, 87)

green fold   of a skirt   green   where
the braided   vine   veering
on   with the flesh   horses
in the skirt   carried   by the ardor
of the light   and   sheep
in the skirt   awakening   flock
interlaced   open to the step   against
the wind   and   swallows   in
the skirt   all of them   are green
today   when the breath
draws   a brown wing   on the edge
of thighs

                     today   nothing
is more than a skirt   in motion

(the skirt   lengthened
by rain   marble
the leg   of a crowd
of young folds)

(*La Quinze chevaux*, 88)

skirt   architecture   softened
by the smoothness   of the belly   by
the invisible   flesh

                                    opaque
and recalcitrant   lining   and   obstinate
in all flesh   a parcel
whose autonomous   flapping
greedily   opens   unto death

body   factory   at night
fall   only a light
can be seen   strident
above   the city
black   between clouds

the skirt   it must be the folds
the folds   smacking
going   doubly
around

(La Quinze chevaux, 89)

but   only able
to circumvent   create
the void   beneath the silk
of the dress   and between
the two banks   within
without support
                     the passage
no geometry   where
the eyes   can rest

no event

the cloth   rustles   like
an ant hill   scintillates
a hive   of flies   on its prey

lights   of the city   taut
veil   over the sky   already
always   black

(La Quinze chevaux, 90)

the body   escapes
even   gored   turned inside out
undone

        except   perhaps
the dead man   abandoned   in a
living   pose   eyes
open   not yet   ready
to forego   existence

A woman   passing
disappeared   and the skirt
at the corner   and the pigeons

no shadow   the ground
walls   dead   stop
of the stone broken by
the opening   of streets
the square   is   empty

(La Quinze chevaux, 91)

THE DISHES

fleeing   bracelets
encircle   wrists of
those hands   under water
elevators   rising
a splash
             water
on the plate   a glimmer
rolls   where eyes
insist   including forks
shifting away   the storm
               yellow
the sponge   scores   the defeat
on the edge   of the saucer
the water   splits   screaming
pit of a fruit   drawn
into the angle   of this slow
               breath
the dish crawls   in the fog
glistens it   waves and banks
united   drops
undone   in the vanishing   plane
               curves
taut   to what turns   runs
happily
             the dishes break
happily

(*La Quinze chevaux*, 92)

the faucet   the benefactor
lunarized   for his encounters
provides   a warm phrase

the water   blue   white
can it be described?
and the constellation   drop
by drop   in the hanging
gardens   as difficult
as the song of   a bird

planes   fly over   the sink
under a tornado   a cyclone
of spoons   ribbons   fax
in the kitchen   the water   blue
white   music   of the generators
if   when   I wash   the dishes
fleeing   bracelets
encircle   wrists of
those hands   under water

elevators   rising
a splash   water   as it turns
drowns   enlivens   the edges
and knows not   if the light
shall hold   all around

(*La Quinze chevaux*, 93)

APPLES

it is   already a murder mystery
when they're put in the basket

              * * *

first of all there's a descent as
of the pole where two precise leaves
move toward the tigrine red of the swelling   then
all is acid green   until the starry orifice
vanishes

they are ingenious—much more so
than leeks or potatoes—
springing forth that way their stems
generating from point to point
back to the umbilic

so   for apples   their bodies escape
unable to weaken the gaze   between
the poles   marking   their hips

(La Quinze chevaux, 94)

with the pear   perhaps   they are
the only fruits   to propose
this unique   access   crunching
biting   really   biting

isn't their   blood
blocked   at a skin level   without pores?

and under the skin   is it the hell of flesh?

biting an apple   a window then opened
on flesh   combustible   given to
air   its whiteness turns   reddish

(*La Quinze chevaux*, 95)

or else   orange red   spiraling
under the blade   pealed skin
falling   balances   the air
then lies down   in the pail

milky womb   joined by marble
the flesh rebels against cartilage
assassinate the apples   kill the dead

spit out the seeds   violet   and a piece
of   dark red skin   in the white   saucer

(La Quinze chevaux, 96)

in the fruit bowl   shutters half-closed
the apples accelerated   the ardor of time

at dusk   an apple on the window
sill   gathered all of day
on its sides

and under an ashen sky   they harvested
the troubling of the storm   turned bluish
then violet   lightly carried
this inexplicable weight

a couple   among   the others ·
had their colors   tarnished
as if by the smoke of an earlier
fire

(*La Quinze chevaux*, 97)

fracas of light   falling on apples

this one seems to be covered by an oily cream
with a reddish scratch   on the hips
sign of the blow   where the dew insisted

in that softness   the brown spot   with
white points   where rot sets in

it is ill equipped   to make it
back up the slope   hopeless   the single
spot of its reddishness   among the green
in the ditch

(La Quinze chevaux, 98)

at the moment   the train passes   throw
an apple   over   the tracks
aiming at the alfalfa field   on the other
side

erotic   this little man   fleshy arms
and short legs   he moves forward
like a rowboat

obese vessel   the apple knocks
with slight tiltings
the tray   off the table

it rolled under the chair
it leans against a shoe
its green leaves barely
grazing   leather

(*La Quinze chevaux*, 99)

what bliss   it would be to die
at the foot   of an apple tree   loaded
down with fruits   to be on one's back   surrounded
by apples   and   above   breaks
in the sky   through   dark
leafage   apples against   cheeks
and thighs   and   believing in
the firmness of their flesh   leaving them
the breath of life

in the room   with metallic furniture
lit up by corridor lights
an apple   might it   help one die
on the night table   it would keep watch
offering the scent of trees   carrying away
in the waves of the orchard whose gates
now close   under a vanishing ceiling

(La Quinze chevaux, 100)

on the riverbanks   farmers   threw
tons of apples   slowly buried
in a sandy bed   trucks
dumped torrents of fruits
and the apples continued their rounds around
their roundness   they hadn't given up
but slid from layer to layer
with powerful smells   edged with the noise
of metallic straps

(*La Quinze chevaux,* 101)

Liliane Giraudon

Photograph by François Lagarde

Liliane Giraudon

Initially: A shock. It was in the south of France, as a child, sitting in the village square at night that I saw (for the very first time) a Charlie Chaplin silent film, where I saw a film within a film—the silent image and its abyss. Then, quite rapidly, around thirteen or fourteen (in a Catholic boarding school, where only Christian books were allowed), I read Racine and Claudel. Then Jouve. Followed by Baudelaire and Dostoyevsky. Finally, Reverdy. They remain as kinds of Monuments. With the packet of misunderstanding that accompanies them. More recently, Robert Walser, Ingeborg Bachmann, Emily Dickinson, Marina Tsvetayeva.

My tastes go toward those "second cuts" of literature, all those who are called "minor" authors, who live in the margins, whose works appear to be off to the side, sidelined, who call for another type of reading, not the one imposed on us by a cultural consensus marked by the times, the epoch, the moment.

I write *under the influence of.* I like the idea of being a woman *under the influence of*—traversed, shoved, cradled by diverse and multiple writings. And yet when I write, I am alone. One writes in order to be alone. That is the contradiction.

I consider the distinctive traits of my poetics precisely those that stand apart from poetry, all the while entertaining a tropistic relation with it. Turned toward it (and a certain modernism insists on denying its existence, and it is true in a sense, "poetry doesn't exist," there is only the line, the poem, the book of poems) like a plant in the direction of light, my writing moves away from it. This is truly a case of attraction-repulsion. A tale of High and Low. All my books of poetry have been constructed according to a principle of Mélange. Most probably because of a desire to safeguard the idea of "the purification of the language" that accompanies all poetic projects. Purification but not cleansing. It is clearly this connotation of purity that distances me from it. Rather than that, I prefer what I have called "Adulterous Mélanges": selections from notebooks, fragments and notes, letters and conversations alternating with poems, separating them and once more allowing them to move forward.

There are no themes in my work. None. Or else those that belong to everybody. If the reader sees them, it is the reader who identifies them through a reading process.

What about being a woman? Does that play in my thinking? As much, no doubt, as it plays within my body, but in ways that are much more complicated and multiple. In any case, there is one thing I am sure of: no writing is gender defined; there is no "feminine writing." Would there be "more . . ." in Desnos or Reverdy than in the Comtesse de Noailles, and "more . . ." in Gertrude Stein or in Ingeborg Bachmann than in Saint-John Perse?

What about women poets not being well represented in anthologies? That's evident. Poetry (much more so than either the novel or the short story) is a Brotherhood [*Fratérie*]. I have a twin brother who, as a child, celebrated Mass. He could do it. He was a boy. Not so in my case. As far as girls were concerned, we were only allowed to change the water in the flower pots before the ceremony. Even today, this memory continues to enlighten me. Is it conceivable (according to the old but always living image of poetry) for a Muse to hold up a Poet, take hold of his poem, and reduce it to its old links (by an act of force) according to a principle of "economy"?

I am now working on an anthology of poetry that will only include women writing and publishing today. [This anthology has appeared.—S. G.]

Poetry at the end of the century? Alive. As Jacques Dupin makes it clear: "It is not, and refuses to be, a literary genre, a cultural artifact, an editorial concept. It is, happily, a loser in marketing calculations. It can neither be reclaimed by computers in the world of publicity nor by programming harrows."

I would add that poetry is in the process of "desacralizing" itself, of leaving the bunker of the Privileged Cult in order to put on a more supple form of dress—in keeping with the world. In this way, it shall resist that general tendency of becoming a cultural ready-to-wear put in place by what Guy Debord calls a "Show society."

What emerges from this object called "poetry" is precisely that it cannot be qualified, that it merits "neither those excessive honors nor those indignities" that envelop it. It follows its own path, pushed around, with variants, inseparable from the destiny of language.

༈

Liliane Giraudon was born in 1946 in Cavaillon and now lives in Marseilles, where she teaches in the public school system. She is a poet, prose writer, cofounder of *Banana Split* and *La Nouvelle Revue B. S.*, and coeditor of the new Marseilles-based magazine *If.* Among her books of poetry are the following:

Têtes ravagées: Une fresque. Paris: La Répétition, 1979.
Je Marche ou je m'endors. Paris: Hachette-Littérature-P.O.L., 1982.
La Réserve. Paris: P.O.L., 1984.
Quel jour sommes-nous. Paris: Ecbolade, 1985.
Divagation des chiens. Paris: P.O.L., 1988.

Among her fiction works are the following:

"La Nuit." Paris: P.O.L., 1986.
Pallaksch, Pallaksch. Paris: P.O.L., 1990. Winner of the Prix Guy de Maupassant.
Fur. Paris: P.O.L., 1992.
Poésies en France depuis 1960: 29 Femmes Poètes, Une Anthologie. Edited by Liliane Giraudon and Henri Deluy. Paris: Stock, 1994.
Les animaux font toujours l'amour de la même manière. Paris: P.O.L., 1995.

Among her works that have been translated into English:

What Day Is It. Translated by Tom Raworth. New York: Women's Studio Workshop, 1986. Reprinted in *Violence of the White Page: Contemporary French Poetry*, edited by Stacy Doris, Phillip Foss, and Emmanuel Hocquard. Special issue of *Tyuonyi*, nos. 9–10 (1991).

Pallaksch, Pallaksch. Translated by Julia Hine. Los Angeles: Sun & Moon, 1994.

Selections from *Pallaksch, Pallaksh*. Translated by Serge Gavronsky. In Serge Gavronsky, *Toward a New Poetics: Contemporary Writing in France*. Berkeley: University of California Press, 1994.

Fur. Translated by Guy Bennet. Los Angeles: Sun & Moon, 1997.

❧

POEM WITH INCENSE PAPER

June 1992–June 1993

Today is summer's day
Light heat and the echo of that voice
The other night   granted   over there
A stroke   a striking stroke
Fingers that black do you remember
about his back

"Is it open late at night?"
"Till morning."

What doesn't move
A rhythmic knot
In sum leaves
Which nothing traverses
Vigor of being
Stop stop yourself
Natural need
Like days egged on
Or eglantines

When there's nothing left to wait for
Tracking a state of being
That thing or another
It's time but no longer
The moment

The heart rinsed out
Wanting to laugh
The meaning of a word

When the answer is in the title
A single reversal
Or a stroke of fate

If by chance you were simply to miss a step
                           For example
I mastered my insomnia from three to six A.M.
Worked up by a wine called "Sang des pierres"
A Vaqueyras slowly drunk near the cry of swifts
Close by the river Sorgue
                          A woman said
I've got a small notebook with a list of my dead friends
When I feel like
Opening it
                          Each word

The expression of a whole life
One of them calls out to me

Why do women call out
More often than men
The word is the name of the place we're speaking from

The women believe in signs
In the numbers of destiny
Our phrases are gestures
(Portrait of Red with or without tulips)

"Don't bury me alive, double check"

It's no longer summer the sun
Is whiter than the white
Of an egg or the back of an eye

Behind the door
Someone was sawing wood

It's like rediscovering point by point
Moments lived through in childhood
Division and separation
Stranger to oneself
Parallel being

What should be
is not necessary

(A rag
doll falling doesn't break)

Behind the window pane
A gray sky lashed suddenly
Turns into a more perfect crimson
When a luminous round spot and
Silent falls trembles above
The hand to the right of the page
Making a hole in the text
Sandy point or severed point

The embroidery must remain flat
You don't know how it shall move
Tiny Yellow Lake lost thread then
Oscillating suddenly falling
Out of the notebook slowly blurring

Into the waxed wood of the table
There are circles hollow
Spots encircled by black or
Somber stringlets

When an invisible knot ceaselessly passes
Enigmatic insects of an enigmatic world
Like looking for the moon
Behind the wall the room

And keeps from the sky
Bodies asleep

When from the river there's no longer
But a rumor of water hawling
Indistinct frozen masses
The fact

of being pushed on with kicks in the ass

Constitutes
A factor too long neglected by
Literary criticism sociology
Of literature and sciences in general

Given that Day Breaks
So it is called named or written down
I see
Behind the curtain acacias
Unique the Red
Of an Apple

As for the sun
Pedal or lever it
Passed through a mass of trees
And it alone and only it
Makes me put down
The book I'm reading

Joseph Conrad's *Heart of Darkness*
Is a rather funereal book
But in truth the more general question linking
Artistic creation
kicks in the ass
Has been neglected

I'm reading *Heart of Darkness*
For the third time
In twenty years and each time
I nearly forget everything
Except the cruelty
A truly psychic abrasion
Similar for example
To vivesecting newborn children

They're treated with curare
Curare immobilizes but does cause sleep
As of that a phenomenon
Similar to the one observed
In adults who have been tortured
Their bodies are white they've just been born
In the book they are black they are adults
But the whites are there
A white man's story

The one which at times disgusts me of being like them
I saw scintillate the Red of an Apple
I thought of the skin of a couple of whites
The very ones who distracted my disgust
Of that color which is mine
A superb gift

I thought of them mingling with the others
Those who now join the list in the notebook
Of a woman near the Sorgue when separation
Like presence is a lily hardly ruffled
I wanted to write a gladiola of those who resist
Violently explode tear apart
The air and go through the seasons
More spoiled than fruits
Resounding on their heads

Were I to tear out my tongue and
Throw it in the fire
Would I then be saved
That's the question I ask you
There's nothing modern about it
And if Sleeping Beauty
Persisted in pricking the same finger
It would only have to be a bit deeper
For the curly haired dog to drink it all
The Lion, the Cat and even the Birds

A tongue in the mouth
Is not the one in books
All books have a spine
Sometimes they crack open
And the leaves fall out
When I cut open a fish
And separate its flesh
On either side of its spinal cord
Am I committing an act of reading

"Gentlemen, you who are
so familiar with the name
of the thing you do, enlighten me"

"You are mistaken confuse everything stop then
Those horrible mélanges clean up clean up more of the literal
Of the objective see Somebody and then Somebody that one here
Not that one there verse has all the privileges except
Not being verse would you then stop liking every
Thing rendering the real is an historic task
Endless technique and private you prefer
Spending hours on the phone going out at night seeing
Movies writing letters to people without
Importance reading stories about werewolves or
Vampires hanging out in bars walking under the
Trees by the sea near the Nile the Tiber or
The Bléonne or any other tributary of any
Which river poetry does not exist etc. . . . etc. . . ."

Far behind the trees one could hear
A real dog, really, bark once
Only once and then keep quiet

You say you're seeking an intensification
A feeling about the whole of existence
Yes the incense paper no longer burns
But its presence remains and since
At times I write in the middle of the day one sleeps
For that solitary exercise I should have a bed
As deep as the Sorgue's
What's the name of the river flowing through Lisbon
It's neither the Neva nor the Don nor the Volga

"*One's got to sleep jot down one's dreams drink*
Gin-Fizzes and stop being afraid"
Says the Weasel to the Coon.

Jacqueline Risset

Photograph by Ermando Di Quinzio

Jacqueline Risset

I really cannot identify "influences," but as for encounters, that's clear enough: sudden encounters make me write. There were three decisive ones at the beginning because, oddly enough, they all acted together, as if the poem to be written found itself somewhere at their intersection, at the intersection of the lines they were drawing in space as they met. (I believe this has always been so for me, as of the beginning, and it is still so today.) The three are Mallarmé, Hölderlin, and Proust. Let me be more specific about each of them.

Mallarmé's posthumous writings: *Anatole's Tomb*, *The Book*, *The Notion*. These were all unfinished texts, fundamental and feverish, where the simplicity of expression had already dealt with every problem, every enigma confronting the act of writing.

Hölderlin, read in Pierre Jean-Jouve's French translations. Here there was the unveiling of new possibilities within language itself: fragments, empty spaces, truly empty between words; his head cracking open; vast landscapes in a single word; and a sudden suspension of meaning, further intensified, as never before, by this very interruption.

And Proust in his 1908 *Notebook*, in a state of urgency, condensed the problem of experience and the book to come—a prodigious energy of thought and image together with a piercing realization of the fragility of the mind containing them.

Just to speak about these texts is already the beginning of an ars poetica, quasi-inaccessible, always present.

I should also include Maurice Scève, that is to say, poetry extracted from a formula much as pearls, as an unapproachable perfection that refuses to deliver its secret and continues to emit mocking astronautic messages: "Come with me, sweet Delia, if you can/Delineate that object for all to see" ["Rejoins-moi si tu peux chère Délie/Délie-moi un peu cet objet pour voir"].

And later on, Petrarch, Bonnefoy's *Douve*, Artaud, Michaux, Pleynet's *Comme*, Sollers's *Drame*, Wallace Stevens, Joyce translated by himself into Italian, Leopardi, and, much later, Dante who gathered in all the threads from Joyce and the Troubadours to Scève and beyond.

As for philosophic encounters—Spinoza: "I finally resolved, I said to myself . . ."; then Heidegger, Nietzsche, Bataille. Psychoanalysis: Freud and Lacan (as writers); and then Ferenczi, Groddeck, Klein, Bion. A negative encounter with Jung (nothing to be learned in that direction—words and things lose their sparkle, their inventiveness, or else fall back into a grayness where everything looks alike and nothing calls out).

Films: a variety, a plasticity in the encounters going from a filmmaker's *oeuvre* to a single image, as if rising to the surface, mysterious object of memory, sometimes perceived as a dreamlike explosion to be questioned and interpreted like a dream, reappearing in a text and walking through it with utmost familiarity.

And Music: as of the beginning, there was always music. I lived in a musical family where, at any moment, you could hear either two instruments being played or my whole family practicing. Music cemented family ties; music was our common language in a French family with strong Republican leanings, together with a sense of discretion (somewhat like Giraudoux's *Tessa* and *Jerome Bardini*). My first poem was composed on the piano. Then we went our separate ways, and yet for me there was always a rhythmic necessity, all things dictated by rhythm. And then the presence of musicians in texts—*Sphere*, Thelonius Monk.

Painting: but then again everything, everything that allows itself to be scanned, everything that changes.

Distinctive Traits: I believe I have always been particularly attentive to beginnings, to birth, to that initial instant when voice throws itself into the void, a crowded void in need of clearing out. In sleep, a weight on one's chest. The weight of language in its entirety to be pushed aside in order to begin. And minimal narratives (the model: the thirty-odd-page narrative in *Maldoror*), single-line or half-line narratives.

THEMES: love, because, every time, it is a pure beginning. The *innamora-mento*, dawn, the emptiness of dawn, vertigo. Or as in the book I am now writing, instants. As if one were actually able to draw up a list of instants and, through that, connect them and, as a consequence, exorcize them as instants, that is, points, emblems of discontinuity in their pure state. Ironic enterprise, to be sure, and rather comical, that is, considering itself as such.

Clearly, if writing presents itself, as of the first experiences, as reflections on one's earliest childhood, as a surprised meditation on identity, at that point, I find the name where I was born. Why here rather than elsewhere? Being a woman presents itself, as of that moment, as a sort of "added turn" given to identity—a supplementary game that defuses and impedes belief. As of that, all passages of identity are felt as immediately impossible and, besides, already secretly attained (Virginia Woolf, *Orlando*); as of the feminine, the masculine is possible, but then so is the mineral. Femininity considered not as continuity, the milk of the Muses, etc., but rather as a form of radical discontinuity, a new birth, absence of property, absence of law. From that, an interesting law—precious, seized from the exterior as an oasis; a reassuring exercise, however slight. The symbolic as a game . . .

About women in anthologies? In this area, I believe there's still much to be done in France. But nothing seems sillier to me than that a priori valorization, vengeful, of a claim for representation in literature. If literature has a meaning, it is obviously in the absence of rules, social rules, a right to identity, the right of a minority, etc. But it is equally obvious that one continues to read racist prejudices. They must be overthrown in order to allow those texts to emerge that until now have been concealed or veiled by such a fault of vision.

I believe that, as we near the end of the century, poetry has an enormous task to perform. It must reconquer and reaffirm its critical and prophetic powers. It can do it.

❧

Jacqueline Risset was born in 1936 in Besançon. She now lives in Rome and teaches at the University of Rome, where she is a professor of French literature. A version of the texts included here and translated by Serge Gavronsky appeared in *Common Knowledge* (fall 1995). Among her publications are the following:

Francis Ponge: Le Parti pris des choses. Italian translation. Rome: Einaudi, 1968.
L'anagramme du désir. Rome: Bulzoni, 1971.
Jeu. Paris: Seuil, 1971.
Mors. Paris: Orange Export, 1976.
La Traduction commence. Paris: Christian Bourgois, 1978.
Dante écrivain. Paris: Seuil, 1982.
Dante, L'Enfer, Le Purgatoire, Le Paradis. Paris: Flammarion, 1985–90.
Sept passages de la vie d'une femme. Paris: Flammarion, 1985.
L'amour de loin. Paris: Flammarion, 1988.
Marcelin Pleynet. Paris: coll. "Poètes d'aujourd'hui," Seghers, 1988.
Petits éléments de physique amoureuse. Paris: coll. "L'infini," Gallimard, 1991.
L'Anagramme du Désir, la Délie de Maurice Scève. Paris: Fourbis, 1995.
Dante, Une vie. Paris: Flammarion, 1995.

Works that have appeared in English:

"Poems." Translated by Rosmarie Waldrop. In *Série d'écriture* 3. London: Spectacular Diseases, 1989.
"Equivalent to Love." Translated by Rosmarie Waldrop. In *Violence of the White Page: Contemporary French Poetry*, edited by Stacy Doris, Phillip Foss, and Emmanuel Hocquard. Special issue of *Tyuonyi*, nos. 9–10 (1991).
"Poems." Translated by Serge Gavronsky. In Serge Gavronsky, *Toward a New Poetics: Contemporary Writing in France.* Berkeley: University of California Press, 1994.
The Translation Begins. Translated by Jennifer Moxley. In *Série d'écriture* 10. Providence, RI: Burning Deck, 1996.

❧

LOVE OF POETRY

It is said that writing serves to keep one at a distance; to
look at emotion from further away. Certainly. But it is also
the opposite: writing serves to heighten life, to make us feel
closer to what one is living—especially when the emotion
coincides, for a time more or less important, with life itself.
Troubadour poets say that "loving" and "singing" are
synonymous verbs. They're right. The one and the other
rises, within sight of each other, as a double wind, aerating
things, changing the landscape. Life, especially when it is lit
up by a new light in the heart, quickly vanishes. One then
madly reaches for a pencil: "Stay, sun, stay for an instant
longer"—a prayer addressed to a piece of paper; but
the star is already on its way. It's a question of instants.

(Petits éléments de physique amoureuse, 9)

INSTANTS I

Of all   instants the most
brilliant the briefest image
is the flash of love

the strongest from childhood
the shock—it is odd,
an absent nymph

crossing receding forests
mirrors
halls of mirrors

The flash appeared as a break
in the secret time of days
  light

I find you again and suddenly
foggy morning
palace peering at the city

I see:
all of life straining toward that point
toward that hollow point

toward that you who is not a being
an absence—
"my children," says the pretty mother

saddened, "you are"
—she finds this curious word: "my unbirth"
and her distress disappears

like a mist—in laughter
whose word? Another mother's, no doubt
she too inventing through memory

and so forth . . .
                    One must be like her
—and without a thing without sadness

Is she happy—is she?
one also rejoices in the approximate
having elementary words

full words   adjectives

rumors of games and adventures
counting one's treasures one's marbles,

—obviously it's something else
in the hollow instant one is nobody
one has nothing nobody

sharp passage of birds   outside
or late in the evening a single swallow
crying—in one's half sleep

a cry aloft,
a trail
and nothing if not

presently after years
                    —situating—
an unknown calm takes care of everything

gracious and discreet in its gestures
the breathing of the ensemble
seen

Here where   I lean I rest
on air
having grasped:
formula for nothing
mortal passage
and that shipwreck

touches me: you see
—but who   are   you?
   perhaps the pretty mother?

Can one love another—another being
apart from life's muted efforts
to be better

muscle in silence hesitation
and solitude
each life an effort

vainly carried by an image
it found on slips of paper
days

remnants of dreams
guiding, invisibly, the fragile
boat

studious glance silent
tender glance   presence
already diverted or dissolved

All words are addressed to him
but they are only unstable clouds
—knowing how to be and then dissolve into rain

ah!   water . . . ah!   sea . . .
ah!   light tempest

"unbirth" . . .

INSTANT II

(Sphere)

Day through
day through and night
gathered
around the same note

and suddenly
—shades, insistent heat
unexpected gallop horses on asphalt

it is the pianist who stops
head aching
and that chord

splendid

insists

That way we enter into the madness of another
he went
mad

and that music

carries him

rather:
he carries
that music come from his mind:
outside . . .

It is the music of   anguishing presence
stopped—suspended
the suspension is beautiful
what frightens is beautiful

An instant later he turns on himself
in the theater
in the airport
a tiny hat holding
his head

he holds around himself
in a circle
approaching forces

though invisible
he throws
at them

in the shadow, hurriedly,

a quick glance and then turns

returns
a bouquet of roses roses
    is a rose

She too is   like you: incapable
of speech
studying her mother tongue in Paris

Thus the poem is born
: out of stupor surprise
and impotency
Stopping on the consonant
of the name St
stopping—

and the opposite:
nocturnal fluid eruption

force within force

the glance weakens—madness
    the body
    in every position

at night the body
under the gaze
forcing

        then the vast stretch—days
        light traces paws on the sand
        pieces found again in the sea

the beautiful car silent
sliding between meadows at dusk
high golden grasses

She does not blush in the wood
in the solitary forest
no longer knowing the way back home

once again she calls back to her childhood
"can you see me?"
"yes"

The music   slows down crystalline
faltering

what it reveals is irrefutable

beyond the window pane

—"ah!   come closer,   explain"

She, distracted,
does not move

—hears, perhaps

SERGE GAVRONSKY was born in Paris, France, in 1932 and came to the United States in 1941. He received his B.A., M.A., and Ph.D. degrees from Columbia University and is the chair of the Department of French at Barnard College, Columbia University, where he was named Olin Professor of French in 1994. His poetry in French and in English has appeared in numerous magazines and anthologies both here and in Japan, France, and Italy. Among his principal publications of poetry are *Lectures et compte-rendu; Même-là, suivi de Geste; Je le suis;* and most recently, *L'interminable discussion.* The author of three novels, all translated into Italian—*The German Friend, The Name of the Father,* and *Identity*—as well as two critical works on twentieth-century French literature, *Culture/Ecriture* and *Ecrire l'homme,* he is also known for his translations of American poets into French, principally the work of Louis Zukofsky, and contemporary French poets into English. His latest work, *Toward a New Poetics: Contemporary Writing in France,* was published in 1994.